SOUND & SYMBOL

The Rudiments of Music

Volume II

David Paul

Faculty of Music, University of Toronto

Royal Conservatory of Music

Canadian Cataloguing in Publication Data

Paul, David, 1948-
  Sound & symbol: the rudiments of music /
David Paul. --

ISBN 0-88797-156-3 (set). — ISBN 0-88797-158-X (v. 1)
ISBN 0-88797-160-1 (v. 2).

1. Music — Theory (Elementary).   I. Title.

MT7.P38   1982   781   C82-095187-0

Published by
The Frederick Harris Music Co., Limited
529 Speers Road
Oakville, Ontario L6K 2G4
416-845-3487

Printed in Canada
F.H. 8405

PREFACE TO VOLUME II

Volume II of *Sound & Symbol* continues the new approach to music rudiments that was begun in *Sound & Symbol*, Volume I. The basic premise of this approach is that students learn theory as they read, play, and sing music. *Sound & Symbol* covers the preliminary, grade I and grade II requirements of the Royal Conservatory of Music. The abbreviations *P, I,* and *II,* which appear in the left-hand margin of the text, indicate the grade level of the topic under discussion. The abbreviation *O* indicates "optional" material that is not required for examination purposes.

Volume II of *Sound & Symbol* covers the following topics: triads, cadences, the expansion and extension of triads, further applications of rhythm and meter (changing time signatures, hybrid meters, and irregular note groups), further means of pitch organization (including chromatic scales), transposition, C clefs, and score study. It includes a substantial amount of material on popular chord symbols, major, minor, and diminished seventh chords, the church modes, pentatonic and whole-tone scales, atonality, and transposing instruments.

The chapters in this volume need not be taught in the exact order shown here, and teachers may choose to present material out of sequence or work on two chapters simultaneously. (For example, I often teach C clefs at the same time as my students are working on another, more involved topic, such as chromatic scales.) However, Chapter 1, *Triads*, should be studied before either Chapter 2, *Cadences*, or Chapter 3, *The Expansion and Extension of Triads*.

I have found that by using the approach presented in *Sound & Symbol*, students gain a knowledge of theory that they can apply directly to their practical work. This accelerates their ability to read, understand, and memorize musical scores. Students who begin the study of harmony after completing Volume II of *Sound & Symbol* are able to harmonize a melody or bass and analyse music much more readily than if their study of rudiments had included only a survey of "the rules". I truly hope that *Sound & Symbol* will make an important difference in the ability of each and every student to appreciate and perform music of many periods and styles.

David Paul

A NOTE ON SIGHT SINGING

Tonic solfa, or the "moveable doh" system, and solfège, or the "fixed do" system, were explained in the Note on Sight Singing in Volume I of *Sound & Symbol*. In Volume II, the presentation of chromatic scales and church modes necessitates further explanation of these approaches to sight singing.

In tonic solfa, the chromatic scale is sung with a different solfa syllable for each note. The chromatic solfa name is derived from the solfa name of the scale note of which the chromatic note is an alteration. Raised scale notes take on an "e" vowel sound. (For example, "doh" raised becomes "de", and "ray" raised becomes "re".) Lowered scale notes take on an "ah" or "oo" vowel sound. (For example, "te" lowered becomes "tah", and "lah" lowered becomes "loo".)

In solfège, the French note names are used for each note of the chromatic scale whether the note is natural, sharp, or flat. When naming notes, a sharpened note is called "dièse" (for example, C sharp is "do dièse"), and a flattened note is called "bémol" (for example, B flat is "si bémol"). However, the words *dièse* and *bémol* are not used in sight singing.

The following chart shows the syllables to sing for a G major chromatic scale in the "moveable doh" and "fixed do" systems.

ASCENDING

	G	G#	A	A#	B	C	C#	D	D#	E	E#	F#	G
	1	#1	2	#2	3	4	#4	5	#5	6	#6	7	1
(Solfège)	sol	sol	la	la	si	do	do	re	re	mi	mi	fa	sol
(Tonic Solfa)	doh	de	ray	re	me	fah	fe	soh	se	lah	le	te	doh

DESCENDING

	G	F#	F	E	Eb	D	Db	C	B	Bb	A	Ab	G
	1	7	b7	6	b6	5	b5	4	3	b3	2	b2	1
(Solfège)	sol	fa	fa	mi	mi	re	re	do	si	si	la	la	sol
(Tonic Solfa)	doh	te	tah	lah	loo	soh	soo	fah	me	mah	ray	rah	doh

The following chart shows the syllables to sing for an E minor chromatic scale in the "moveable doh" and "fixed do" systems.

ASCENDING

	E	E#	F#	G	G#	A	A#	B	C	C#	D	D#	E
	1	#1	2	3	#3	4	#4	5	6	#6	7	#7	1
(Solfège)	mi	mi	fa	sol	sol	la	la	si	do	do	re	re	mi
(Tonic Solfa)	lah	le	te	doh	de	ray	re	me	fah	fe	soh	se	lah

DESCENDING

	E	D#	D	C#	C	B	Bb	A	Ab	G	F#	F	E
	1	#7	7	#6	6	5	b5	4	b4	3	2	b2	1
(Solfège)	mi	re	re	do	do	si	si	la	la	sol	fa	fa	mi
(Tonic Solfa)	lah	se	soh	fe	fah	me	mah	ray	rah	doh	te	tah	lah

The church, or ecclesiastical, modes are related through structural similarities to major and natural minor scales. The Ionian mode uses the same pattern of tones and semitones as a major scale. The tonic solfa syllables for a scale in the Ionian mode are as follows:

1	2	3	4	5	6	7	8
doh	ray	me	fah	soh	lah	te	doh

The Lydian mode is identical in structure to a major scale with sharpened 4th degree.

1	2	3	#4	5	6	7	8
doh	ray	me	fe	soh	lah	te	doh

The Mixolydian mode is identical in structure to a major scale with flattened 7th degree.

1	2	3	4	5	6	b7	8
doh	ray	me	fah	soh	lah	tah	doh

The Aeolian mode uses the same pattern of tones and semitones as a natural minor scale.

1	2	3	4	5	6	7	8
lah	te	doh	ray	me	fah	soh	lah

The Dorian mode is identical in structure to a natural minor scale with sharpened 6th degree.

1	2	3	4	5	#6	7	8
lah	te	doh	ray	me	fe	soh	lah

The Phrygian mode is identical in structure to a natural minor scale with flattened 2nd degree.

1	b2	3	4	5	6	7	8
lah	tah	doh	ray	me	fah	soh	lah

When singing modal melodies using the "fixed do" system, the student simply sings the French name for each melody note, without including the words "dièse" and "bémol" for notes that are altered.

ACKNOWLEDGEMENTS

The author wishes to acknowledge permission to reprint the following copyright material:

An excerpt from Gustav Holst's "Neptune the Mystic" from *The Planets*, Op. 29. Copyright J. Curwen & Sons Ltd. Reproduced by permission.

Excerpts from Sergei Prokofiev's Violin Concerto No. 2, Op. 63, and Igor Stravinsky's *Petrouchka* and *The Rite of Spring*. Copyright Boosey & Hawkes Inc. Reproduced by permission.

John Beckwith's "The Man of Thessaly" from *Ten English Rhymes*. Copyright 1964 BMI Canada Limited. Used by permission of Berandol Music Limited.

An excerpt from Jean Sibelius's *Karelia Suite*. © by Breitkopf & Haertel, Wiesbaden.

Yannis Constantinidis's *Greek Miniature, No. 13*. © Copyright 1951 by Yannis Constantinidis. All rights for the world, outside of Greece, assigned to Rongwen Music, Inc. © Copyright 1957 by Rongwen Music, Inc. Used by permission of the copyright holder.

Two excerpts from Manuel de Falla's *El Amor Brujo*. Used by kind permission of J & W Chester/Edition Wilhelm Hansen London Limited.

English words to "My Bark Canoe" from *American Primitive Music* by Frederick R. Burton. Reprinted by permission of the publisher, Dodd, Mead & Company, Inc.

Excerpts from Harry Somer's *Fantasia for Orchestra* and Claude Champagne's *Symphonie gaspésienne*. Used by permission of Berandol Music Limited.

An excerpt from Harry Freedman's *Variations for Flute, Oboe, and Harpsichord*. Used by permission of the composer.

An excerpt from Jean Coulthard's "The Star Shone Down". Used by permission of Jaymar Music Limited.

An excerpt from John Weinzweig's "To the Lands Over Yonder". Copyright 1953, John Weinzweig. Reprinted by permission.

"She's Like the Swallow" from *Folk Songs from Newfoundland*, collected by Maud Karpeles. By permission of Oxford University Press.

In addition, the author would like to acknowledge the source of John McCrae's "In Flanders Fields", first published in *Punch* magazine.

CONTENTS

4. *FURTHER APPLICATIONS OF METER AND RHYTHM*

Sound & Symbol

Volume II

1. TRIADS

Trio (No. 16) from Die Zauberflöte

Wolfgang Amadeus Mozart
(1756-1791)

Allegretto

Seid uns zum zwei - ten Mal will - kom - men, ihr Män - ner in_____ Sa-
This is the se - cond time we meet you This time in great_____ Sa-

ra - stro's Reich! Er schickt, was man___ euch ab - ge - nom - men,
ra - stro's realm. He has com - mand - ed that___ we greet you,

die Flö - te und die_ Glöckchen euch. Wollt ihr die Spei - sen nicht_ver-schmä-hen,
and flute and bells, to___ now___ re - turn. Now at the ta - ble there_ be seat-ed,

so es - set, trin - ket froh___ da - von! Wenn wir zum drit - ten
and eat and drink so glad - ly there. When for the third___ time

This vocal trio for three boys — No. 16 from Mozart's opera *The Magic Flute* — is in a three-part texture. (In Mozart's original score, these three vocal parts are provided with an orchestral accompaniment.)

When three or more notes are played or sung simultaneously, the resulting sound is called a *chord*. Certain types of three-note chords are called *triads*.

INTRODUCTION TO TRIADS

P I II **Triads in Root Position**

A triad is a type of three-note chord. A triad is in root position when adjacent notes are a 3rd apart. The lowest note is called the *root*. The middle note, a 3rd above the root, is called the *third*. The uppermost note, which is a 5th above the root (a 3rd above the third), is called the *fifth*.

This is a triad built on G.
The root is G. The third is B.
The fifth is D.

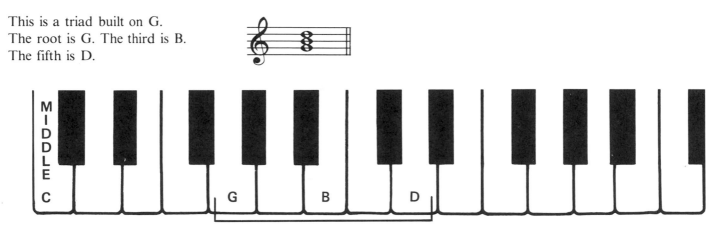

This is a triad built on C.
The root is C. The third is E.
The fifth is G.

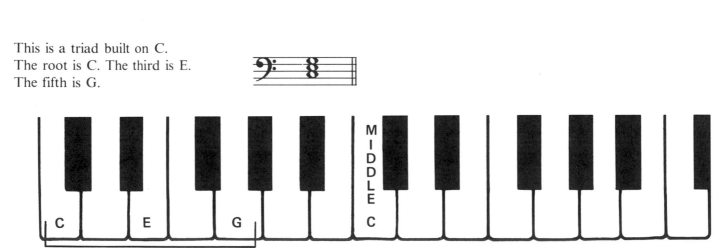

Tonic and Dominant Triads

A triad can be built on any degree of a major or minor scale. The tonic and dominant triads — those built on the tonic and dominant notes of the scale — are the most important. The *degree* of the scale on which a triad is built is symbolized by means of a Roman numeral — "I" for the tonic triad and "V" for the dominant triad.

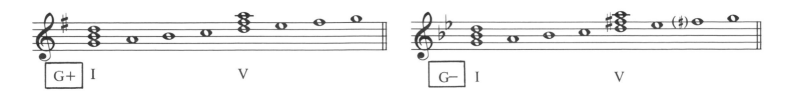

As you learned in Volume I of *Sound & Symbol,* an interval is categorized as major, minor, augmented, or diminished, according to its type or quality. Since a triad is composed of intervals, its quality depends on the intervals it contains. All of the following triads have C as their root, yet each has a different quality.

A *major* triad consists of a major 3rd (from root to third), and a perfect 5th (from root to fifth). As with intervals, the symbol for major is "+". Each of the following triads is major. The third and fifth of each triad are in the major scale of the root (the lowest note).

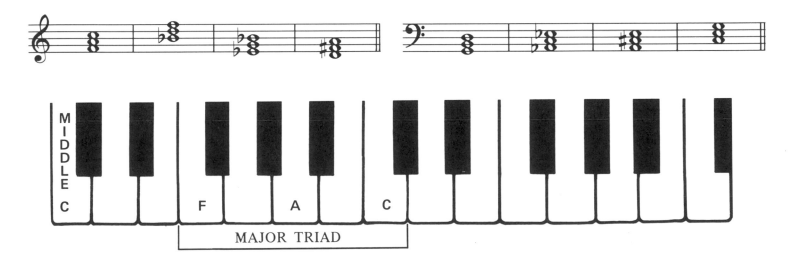

A *minor* triad consists of a minor 3rd (from root to third), and a perfect 5th (from root to fifth). As with intervals, the symbol for minor is "–". Each of the following triads is minor. The third and fifth of each triad are in the minor scale of the root (the lowest note).

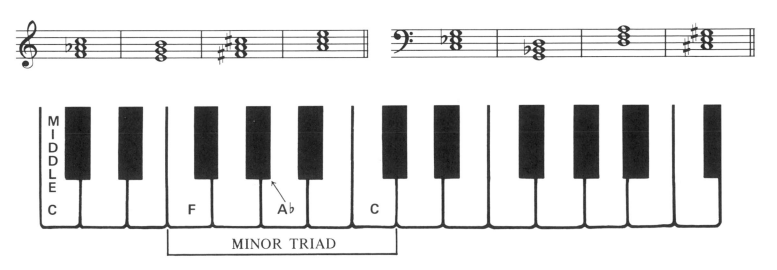

Inversions of Triads

A triad is said to be inverted when its root is not the lowest note. If the third of the chord is the lowest note, the triad is in *first inversion*. If the fifth is the lowest note, the triad is in *second inversion*. Study these examples.

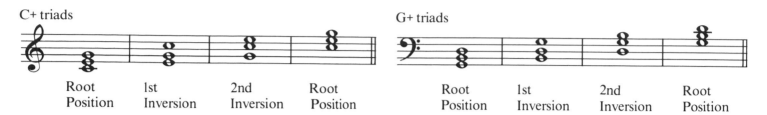

C+ triads				G+ triads			
Root Position	1st Inversion	2nd Inversion	Root Position	Root Position	1st Inversion	2nd Inversion	Root Position

The *position* of a triad is indicated by means of Arabic numerals that refer to the intervals between the upper notes of the triad and the lowest note. Root position is expressed by the figure $\frac{5}{3}$, first inversion by the figure $\frac{6}{3}$, and second inversion by the figure $\frac{6}{4}$.

There are several registers in which a triad can be placed. The following are all root position C+ triads:

These are all first inversion C+ triads:

These are all second inversion C+ triads:

A triad is analysed by specifying its root, quality and position.

The following is an A+ triad in root position:

This is a G– triad in second inversion:

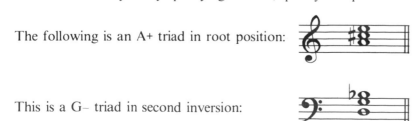

Solid and Broken Triads

Triads are most often associated with the harmonic aspect of music, but they can also be used melodically. A triad is said to be in *solid* form when the three notes are sounded simultaneously, and in *broken* form when the notes are sounded one after the other in a linear, or melodic, manner.

F+ solid triads: F+ broken triads:

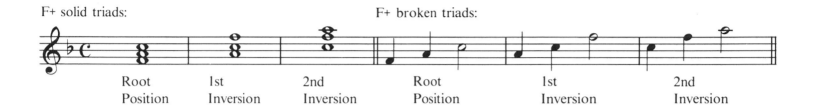

| Root Position | 1st Inversion | 2nd Inversion | Root Position | 1st Inversion | 2nd Inversion |

Broken triads are an integral part of many melodies. Study the analysis of broken triads in the following examples.

W.A. Mozart

Root	F			Bb
Quality	+			+
Position	5/3			5/3

J.S. Bach

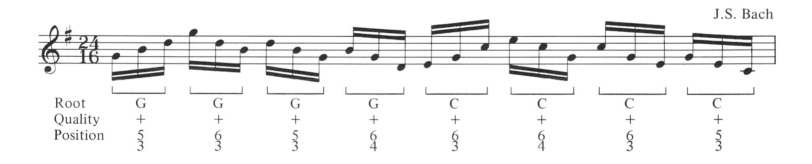

Root	G	G	G	G	C	C	C	C
Quality	+	+	+	+	+	+	+	+
Position	5/3	6/3	5/3	6/4	6/3	6/4	6/3	5/3

B. Galuppi

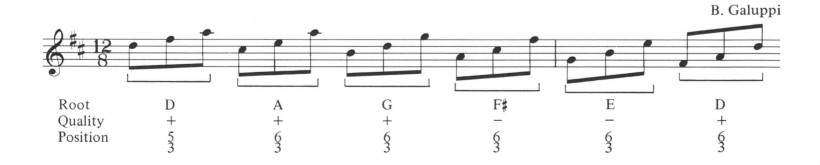

Root	D	A	G	F#	E	D
Quality	+	+	+	−	−	+
Position	5/3	6/3	6/3	6/3	6/3	6/3

Three-Part Song

Sing (or sing and play) this three-part setting of a Canadian folk song as a practical introduction to the sound of triadic harmony. Notice the difference in sound between major triads and minor triads, and between root positions and inversions. Notice also the four places where the texture has been reduced to either two parts or one.

À la claire fontaine

Slowly and Pensively   Canada

A la clai - re fon - tai - ne M'en al - lant pro - me - ner,
At the clear run - ning brook - let I stopped up - on my way.

J'ai trou - vé l'eau si bel - le Que je m'y suis bai - gné.____
I found the stream so cool - ing, I swam that sum - mer day.____

Lui ya long - temps que je t'ai - me, Ja - mais je ne t'ou - blie - rai.
Now man - y years have I loved you, Al - ways in my heart you'll stay.

P I II EXERCISES ON TONIC AND DOMINANT TRIADS

1. Name the root, third and fifth of each of the following triads.

Fifth ____ ____ ____ ____ ____ ____ ____ ____
Third ____ ____ ____ ____ ____ ____ ____ ____
Root ____ ____ ____ ____ ____ ____ ____ ____

2. For each of the following scales:
   (i) name the key;
   (ii) build triads on the tonic and dominant notes;
   (iii) symbolize the triads as tonic or dominant.

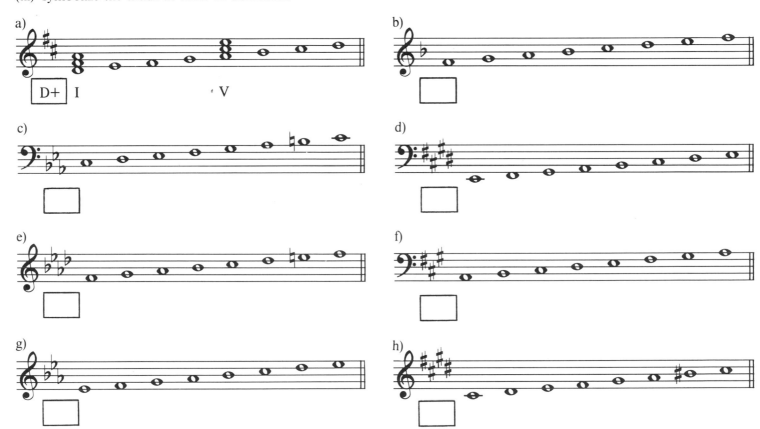

a) D+ | I   'V

3. For each of the following triads:
   (i) name the key;
   (ii) symbolize the triads as tonic or dominant.

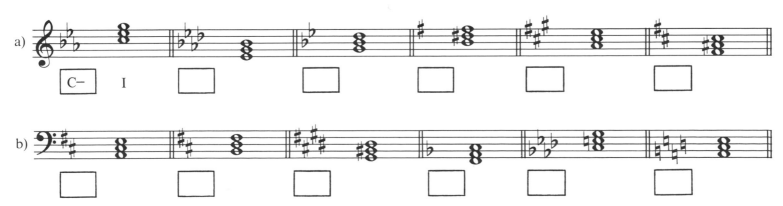

a) C− | I

b)

4. Write the following triads in the treble clef, using the correct key signature for each.

| E+ | I | G− | V | F♯− | V | A♭+ | I | C− | I |

5. Write the following triads in the bass clef, using the correct key signature for each.

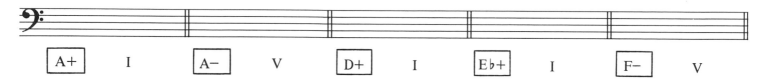

| A+ | I | A− | V | D+ | I | E♭+ | I | F− | V |

P I II [EXERCISES ON MELODIC UNITS]

1. For each of the following melodies:
   (i) name the key;
   (ii) play the melody with the right hand while accompanying with tonic and dominant triads in the left hand;
   (iii) write the appropriate symbol for each tonic and dominant triad on the lines provided.

England

e)

Russia

f)

Poland

g)

I II EXERCISES ON MAJOR AND MINOR TRIADS AND THEIR INVERSIONS

1. Add the symbols "+" and "−" to indicate whether each of the following triads is major or minor. Play each triad.

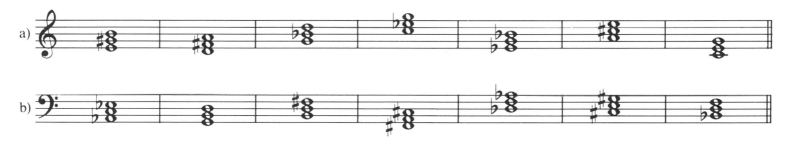

a)

b)

2. Write, then sing the notes that form a *major* triad above each of the following.

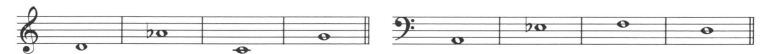

3. Write, then sing the notes that form a *minor* triad above each of the following.

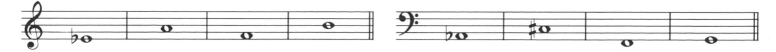

4. Add accidentals where necessary to make the following triads *major*. Play each triad.

5. Add accidentals where necessary to make the following triads *minor*. Play each triad.

6. For each of the following examples:
(i)   write a *major* triad in root position above the given note;
(ii) write the two inversions of this triad;
(iii) play the triads you have written.

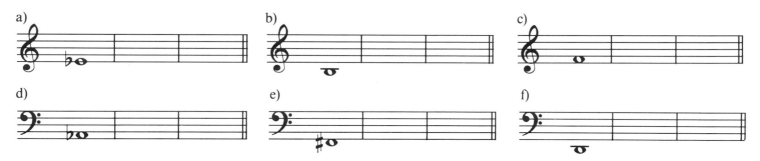

7. For each of the following examples:
(i)   write a *minor* triad in root position above the given note;
(ii) write the two inversions of this triad;
(iii) play the triads you have written.

8. Write, then sing the notes that form a first inversion *major* triad above each of the following.

9. Write, then sing the notes that form a first inversion *minor* triad above each of the following.

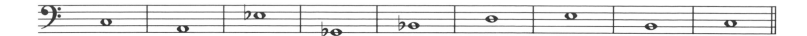

10. Write, then sing the notes that form a second inversion *major* triad above each of the following.

11. Write, then sing the notes that form a second inversion *minor* triad above each of the following.

12. For each of the following triads:
    (i) add accidentals to make the triad *major;*
    (ii) name the position;
    (iii) name the *minor* key of which it is the dominant triad.

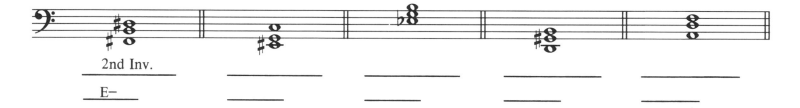

    2nd Inv.

    E–

I II   EXERCISES ON MELODIC UNITS AND THREE-PART TEXTURES

1. For each of the following thematic excerpts containing broken triads:
   (i) name the root, quality and position of each bracketed triad;
   (ii) play the excerpt.

Gavotte from Colinette à la cour

A. Grétry

14

Piano Sonata No. 14, ("Moonlight"), 1st mvt.

Minuet, K. 2

Piano Sonata No. 31, 1st mvt.

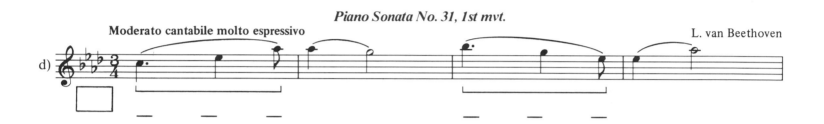

Piano Sonata No. 26 ("Les Adieux"), 3rd mvt.

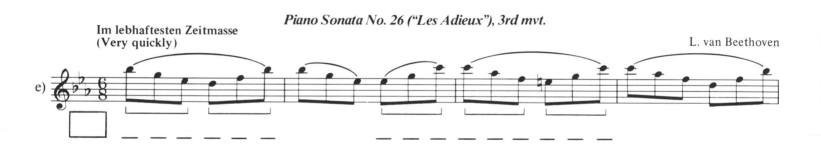

Concerto Grosso, Op. 6, No. 10, 5th mvt.

Piano Sonata No. 13, 2nd mvt.

2. The first triad of each of the following *major* mode trios has been analysed. Analyse each new triad or new position of a triad by specifying its root, type and position. Play each trio. Prepare one trio for a three-part vocal performance with two fellow students.

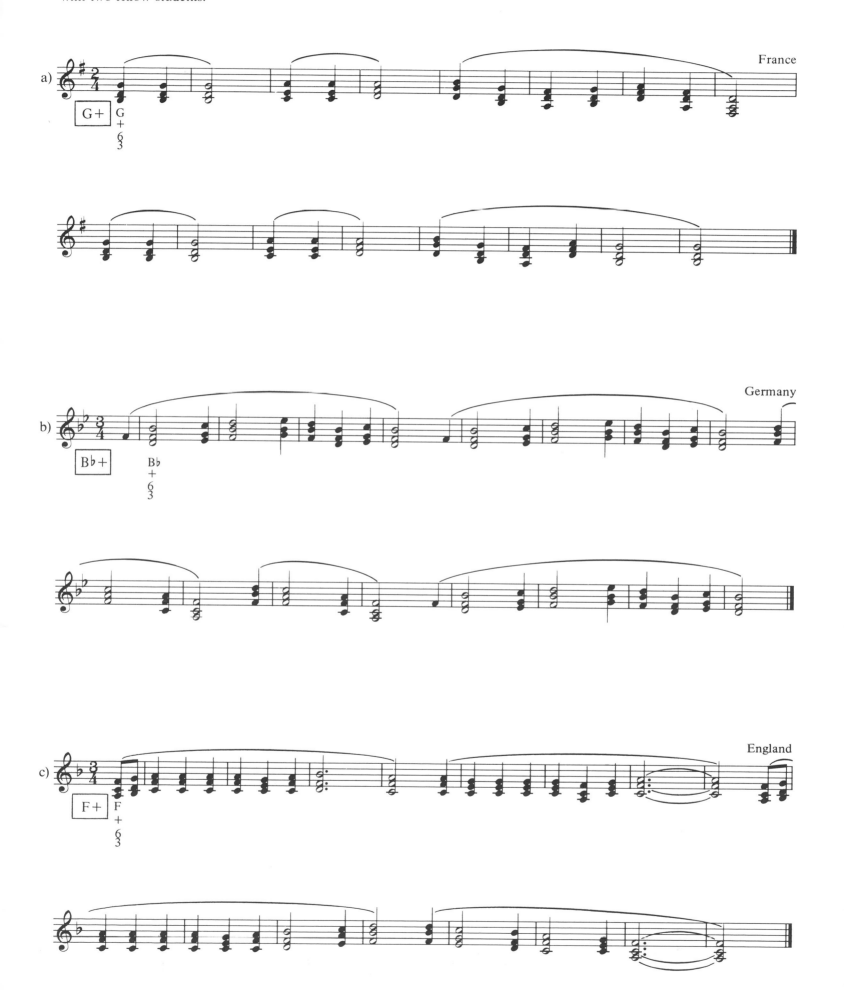

3. The first triad of each of the following *minor* mode trios has been analysed. Analyse each new triad or new position of a triad by specifying its root, type and position. Play each trio. Prepare one trio for a three-part vocal performance with two fellow students.

a)

A–   A
     —
     6
     3

England

b)

G–   G
     —
     6
     4

Finland

c)

F♯–   F♯
      —
      6
      3

Czechoslovakia

4. The following excerpt from an orchestral work by Debussy is an example of a three-part texture. In Debussy's original score, the three parts are played by three trumpets, which are accompanied by other instruments. Analyse the triads by specifying the root, type and position wherever lines are provided.*

Fêtes from Nocturnes

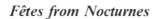

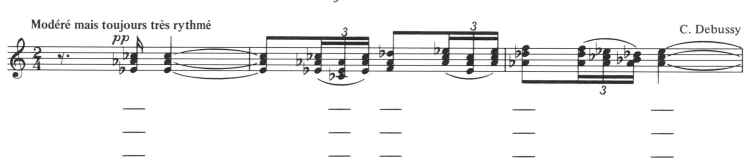

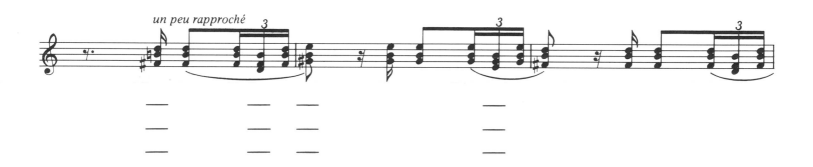

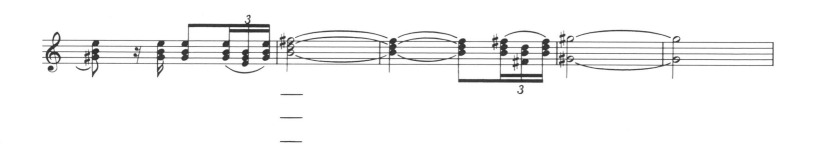

*The triplet rhythm ( ) will be explained in Chapter 4.

FURTHER CONCEPTS OF TRIADS

Augmented and Diminished Triads

An *augmented* triad consists of a major 3rd (from root to third) and an augmented 5th (from root to fifth). As with intervals, the symbol for augmented is "**x**". The following are all augmented triads.

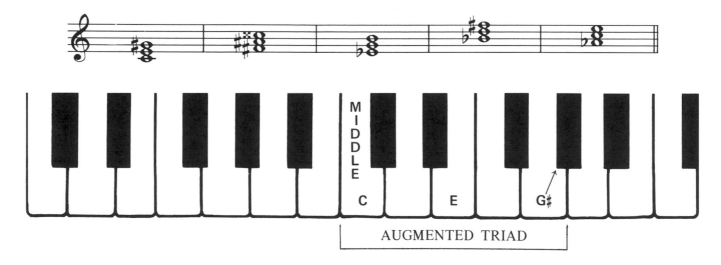

AUGMENTED TRIAD

A *diminished* triad consists of a minor 3rd (from root to third) and a diminished 5th (from root to fifth). As with intervals, the symbol for diminished is "**○**". The following are all diminished triads.

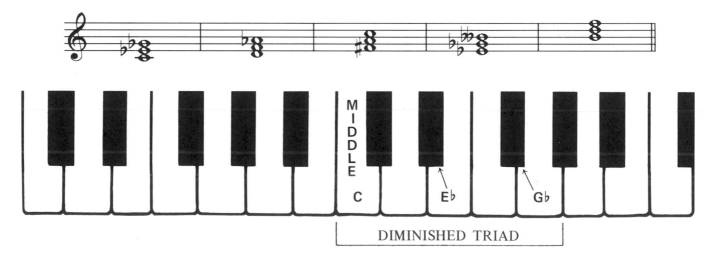

DIMINISHED TRIAD

Augmented and diminished triads are inverted in the same way that major and minor triads are inverted. In first inversion, the third is the lowest note. In second inversion, the fifth is the lowest note.

Piano Piece with Augmented and Diminished Triads

The following passage is a simplification of a piano piece by Edvard Grieg. It contains one augmented and two diminished chords. Play the melody on the piano with your right hand, accompanying it with the chords given in the left hand. Notice that the augmented and diminished triads have a strong tendency to pull toward the next chord.

Norwegian Dance, Op. 35, No. 2

Edvard Grieg
(1843-1907)

Open Position of Triads

The triads you have studied to this point have all been in "close position". In other words, the three notes of each triad have been written as closely together as possible.

A triad is in "open position" when its notes are *not* written as closely together as possible and are therefore *not* contained within the range of a 5th (in root position) or within that of a 6th (in first or second inversion).

In the following example, open position triads appear directly beneath the close position triads on which they are based.

Close Position:

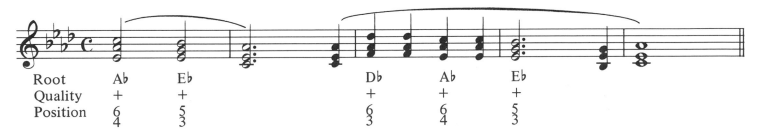

Root	Ab	Eb		Db	Ab	Eb	
Quality	+	+		+	+	+	
Position	6/4	5/3		6/3	6/4	5/3	

Open Position:

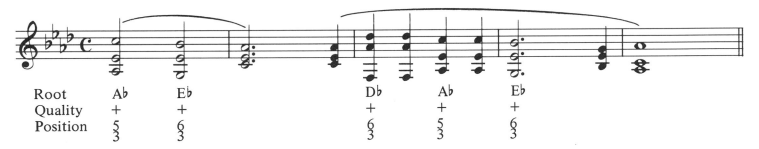

Root	Ab	Eb		Db	Ab	Eb	
Quality	+	+		+	+	+	
Position	5/3	6/3		6/3	5/3	6/3	

Notice that when a triad appears in open position, its lowest note still indicates whether it is in root position, first inversion, or second inversion. If the root is the lowest note, the triad is in *root position*. If the third is the lowest note, the triad is in *first inversion*. If the fifth is the lowest note, the triad is in *second inversion*.

O   ## *Implied Triads*

A three-part texture may occasionally reduce to two parts. This two-part sonority can suggest a triad. Usually the root and third, or less frequently the root and fifth, imply the complete triad. Music in three parts can also imply a triad when two roots and a third, or two roots and a fifth, appear in place of the root, third and fifth. The final chord of the example shown above illustrates an implied triad. It contains a root, a third, and another root (Ab, C, Ab) rather than a root, third and fifth (Ab, C, Eb).

II | *Three-Part Song*

Sing (or sing and play) this three-part song as an introduction to the sound of a piece using augmented and diminished triads as well as major and minor triads. This arrangement contains triads in root position, triads in first inversion, and triads in second inversion. Some of these triads are in close position, others are in open position.

Sleep, Baby, Sleep

Luise Reichardt
(arr. David Paul)

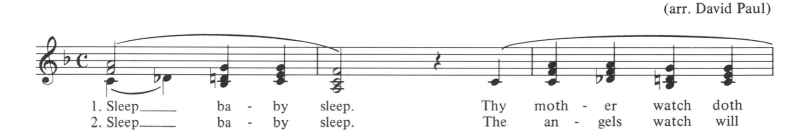

1. Sleep_____ ba - by sleep. Thy moth - er watch doth
2. Sleep_____ ba - by sleep. The an - gels watch will

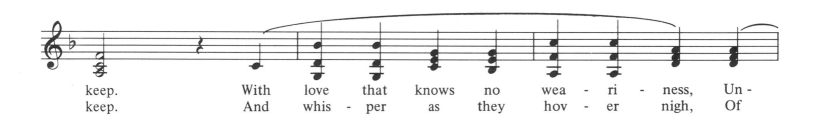

keep. With love that knows no wea - ri - ness, Un -
keep. And whis - per as they hov - er nigh, Of

tir - ing in its ten - der - ness. Sleep___ ba - by sleep.
heav'n - ly love be - yond the sky. Sleep___ ba - by sleep.

Finding All Keys Containing a Given Triad

When a question asks, "Find all the keys containing the triad D, F♯ and A ( )", it is really asking

you to find all the major and *harmonic* minor scales that contain these three notes. To answer this question:

1) List, in chart form, all the major and minor keys.

Flat Keys		No Key Signature		Sharp Keys	
F+	D–	C+	A–	G+	E–
B♭+	G–			D+	B–
E♭+	C–			A+	F♯–
A♭+	F–			E+	C♯–
D♭+	B♭–			B+	G♯–
G♭+	E♭–			F♯+	D♯–
C♭+	A♭–			C♯+	A♯–

2) Exclude all keys that do not contain D, which is the root of the triad. (In other words, exclude keys that contain the notes D♯ or D♭.) The following keys remain:

F+	D–	C+	A–	G+	
B♭+	G–			D+	B–
E♭+	C–			A+	F♯–
	E♭–				

3) Exclude all keys that do not contain F♯, the third of the triad. (In other words, exclude any key that has F or F♭.) The following keys remain:

G–	G+	
	D+	B–
	A+	F♯–

4) Exclude all keys that do not contain A, the fifth of the triad. (In other words, exclude any key that has A♭ or A♯.) The following keys remain:

G–	G+	
	D+	
	A+	F♯–

The keys that contain the triad of D major are therefore G+, G–, D+, A+, and F♯–.

Traditional Chord Symbols

You have already learned that in any key, major or minor, triads can be built on the tonic and dominant notes of the scale, and that these triads are of primary importance in a key. Triads can also be built on other degrees of a scale. Like the tonic and dominant triads, they take their names from the scale degrees on which they are built. The triad on the 2nd degree is known as the *supertonic* triad, that on the 3rd degree is called the *mediant* triad, and that on the 4th degree is called the *subdominant* triad. The 6th and 7th degree triads are known as the *submediant* and *leading-note* triads respectively.

Study the following examples of triads built on the various degrees of the major and minor scales. Observe that in the traditional system of symbolizing triads within a key, Roman numerals are used to specify the scale degree on which each triad is built. In major keys, triads built on I, IV and V are major, triads built on II, III and VI are minor, and the triad built on VII is diminished. In minor keys, triads built on V and VI are major, triads built on I and IV are minor, triads built on II and VII are diminished, and the triad built on III is augmented.* *The type of triad found on each degree of a major scale is the same for all major scales, just as the type of triad found on each degree of a harmonic minor scale is the same for all harmonic minor scales.*

Examples:

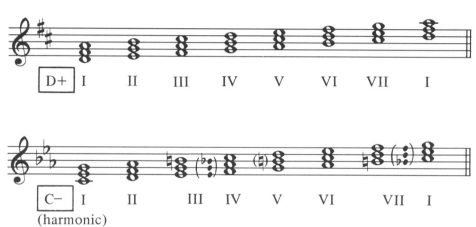

Here are two short examples of triadic harmony with traditional chord symbols placed beneath.

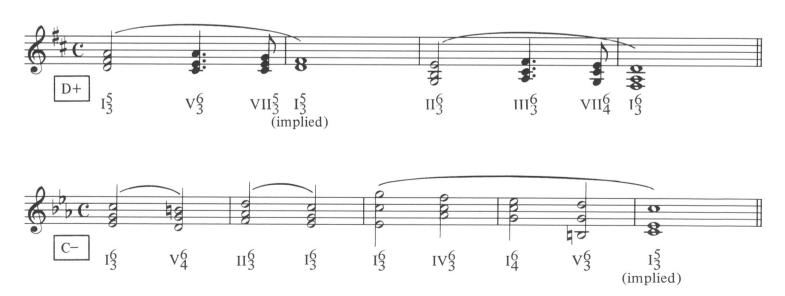

*Of the three forms of the minor scale (natural, harmonic, and melodic), the harmonic is the one most frequently drawn upon to create chords in the minor mode. In addition, major chords on III and VII from the natural minor or descending melodic minor scale are also encountered in composed music.

O **Popular Chord Symbols**

In popular music, musicians often play from *charts* rather than from completely written-out musical compositions. These charts, or *lead sheets,* contain the melody, the words (in the case of vocal music), and *popular chord symbols.* From these chord symbols, the musicians create their accompaniment to the melody.

A capital letter such as **G** written above a lead sheet melody indicates that a major triad with root G (G, B, D) should be played in root position as accompaniment. A capital letter with a small **m** after it, such as **Gm**, indicates that a minor triad with root G (G, B♭, D) should be played in root position as accompaniment. If any note *other* than the root of the chord is to be played as the lowest, this note is indicated by a second capital letter preceded by a slash. Thus, **Gm/D** symbolizes a G minor triad with D as the lowest note.

Examples:

In the system of popular chord symbols, the augmented triad is symbolized by a capital letter representing the root of the chord, followed by **aug** or x. The diminished chord is symbolized by a capital letter representing the root of the chord, followed by **dim** or ○.

Examples:

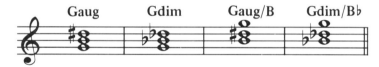

The next example is a lead sheet of a song. The lower staff contains the triads designated by the popular chord symbols. Play the melody on the piano with your right hand and the accompanying chords with your left hand. (Notice that from the 4th to the 6th complete bar, the left-hand part plays parallel triads. Although these would be forbidden in the traditional harmonic style of "classical" music, they are nevertheless quite common and fully acceptable in folk and popular music.)

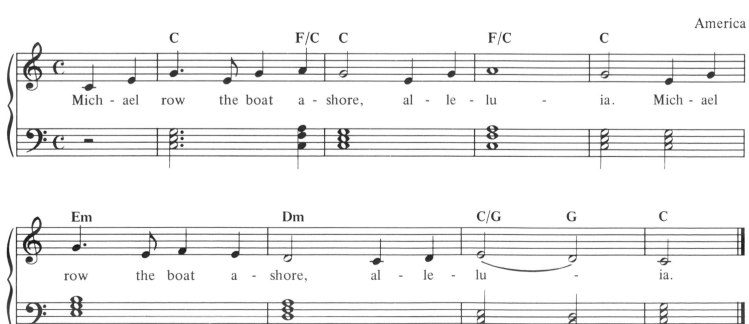

II EXERCISES ON TRIADS

1. Analyse each of the following triads by specifying its root, quality and position.

Example:

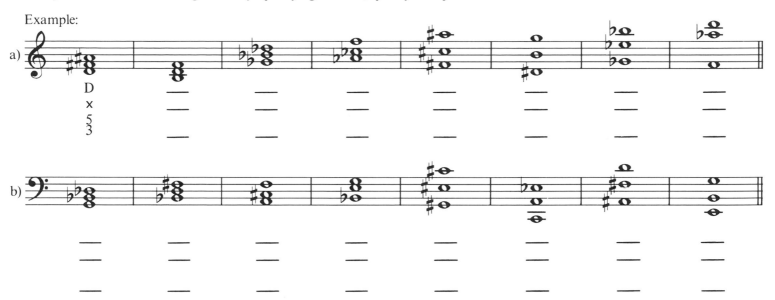

2. For each of the following examples:
   (i) write a diminished triad in root position above the given note;
   (ii) write the two inversions of this triad;
   (iii) play the triads you have written.

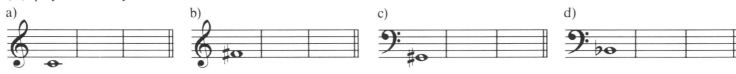

3. For each of the following examples:
   (i) write an augmented triad in root position above the given note;
   (ii) write the two inversions of this triad;
   (iii) play the triads you have written.

4. Name all the keys that contain the following triads:

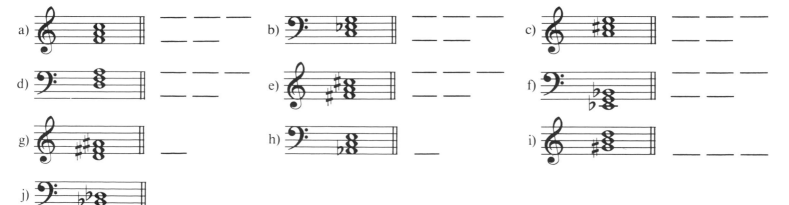

26

5. Name the one triad found in all of the following keys: E+, B+, A+, G♯–, and A–. _____

6. Name the one triad found in all of the following keys: F–, C–, E♭+, D♭+, and A♭+. _____

7. Name the one triad common to these three keys: E+, E–, and C♯–. _____

8. Name the one triad found only in the key of D–. _____

9. For each of the following major scales:
   (i) write a triad on each note, using only notes from the scale;
   (ii) label each triad with its traditional chord symbol.

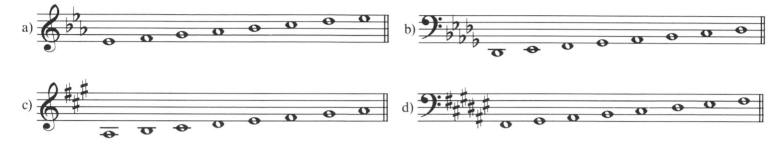

10. For each of the following harmonic minor scales:
   (i) write a triad on each note, using only notes from the scale;
   (ii) label each triad with its traditional chord symbol.

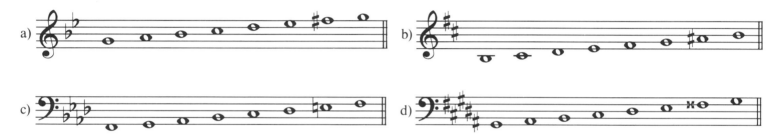

11. For each of the following triads:
   (i) name the key;
   (ii) label the triad with its traditional chord symbol.

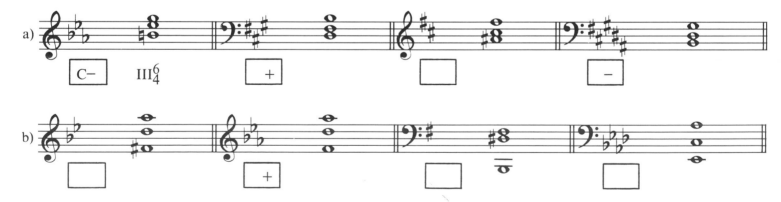

12. Write close position triads in each of the following keys according to the given symbols.

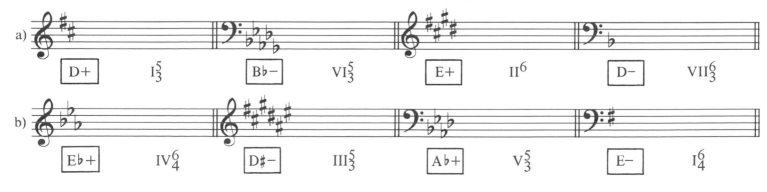

II EXERCISES ON MELODIC UNITS AND THREE-PART TEXTURES

1. Each of the following thematic excerpts contains one or more broken triads. Specify the root, quality and position of each bracketed triad.

2. For each of the following trios:
   (i) name the key;
   (ii) play the trio;
   (iii) circle and label ("×" or "○") all examples of augmented or diminished triads, and specify the root and position of each.

England

Bavaria

3. Analyse the triads in the following excerpts by specifying the root, quality and position wherever lines are provided.

Prélude from Pour le piano

C. Debussy

Dance of the Toy Flutes from The Nutcracker

P.I. Tchaikovsky

4. This "Chorus of Priests" from Mozart's opera *The Magic Flute* is an example of three-part texture. (The orchestral accompaniment has been omitted.) Play the three vocal parts on the piano.* Analyse the triads by specifying the root, quality and position wherever lines are provided.

Wolfgang Amadeus Mozart
(1756-1791)

*Tenor parts should be performed one octave lower than written.

5. For each of the following trios:
  (i) name the key;
 (ii) play the trio;
(iii) label each triad with its *traditional* chord symbol.

Flanders

b)

o

Further Exercises

1. For each of the following lead sheets:
   (i) on the staff provided, write the close position triads designated by the given popular chord symbols;
   (ii) play the melody along with the triadic accompaniment you have written.

Symphony No. 9 ("From the New World"), 2nd mvt.

A. Dvořák

Go Down, Moses

America

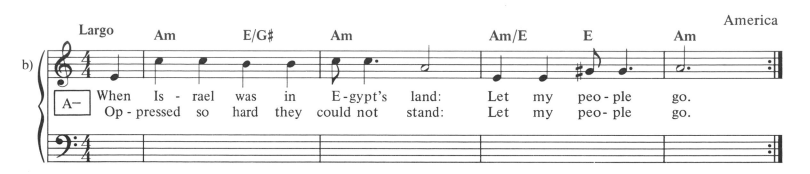

When Is - rael was in E - gypt's land: Let my peo - ple go.
Op - pressed so hard they could not stand: Let my peo - ple go.

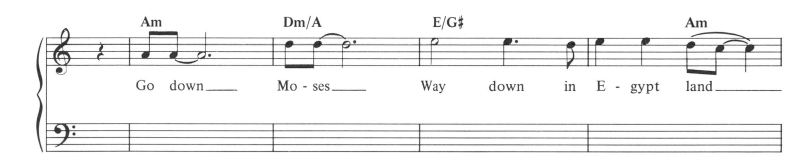

Go down___ Mo - ses___ Way down in E - gypt land___

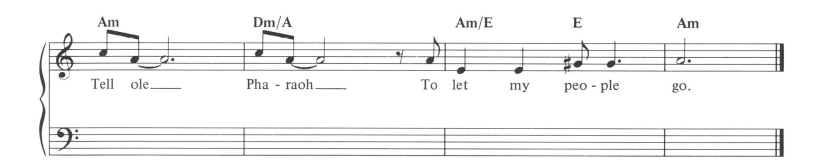

Tell ole___ Pha - raoh___ To let my peo - ple go.

2. CADENCES

Symphony No. 5, 1st mvt.
(conclusion)

Ludwig van Beethoven
(1770-1827)

The term *cadence* is used to describe a pair of chords that provides musical punctuation. In the first movement of his Symphony No. 5, Beethoven achieves a particularly convincing sense of punctuation by repeating dominant and tonic chords several times before the final cadence.

I II

TYPES OF CADENCES

Final and Non-final Cadences

A cadence is a musical idiom consisting of two adjacent chords that support a melody at the end of a phrase. There are essentially two types of cadence, *final* and *non-final*.

A *final cadence* can be used to complete a musical phrase or section, or an entire composition. The last chord of a final cadence is always the tonic triad. The first chord of a final cadence can be either the dominant or the subdominant triad. The cadential progression V–I (dominant to tonic) is called a *Perfect Cadence*. The Perfect Cadence is the most commonly found final cadence in music. The cadential progression IV–I (subdominant to tonic) is called a *Plagal Cadence*. The Plagal Cadence is often used to set the word "Amen" at the end of a hymn.

A *non-final cadence* can be used to end a phrase or section of a piece of music, but is less conclusive than a final cadence. For this reason, a non-final cadence is not used to end a musical composition. The second chord of a non-final cadence is always V. The first chord can be I, II, IV or VI. Non-final cadences are referred to as *Imperfect Cadences*.

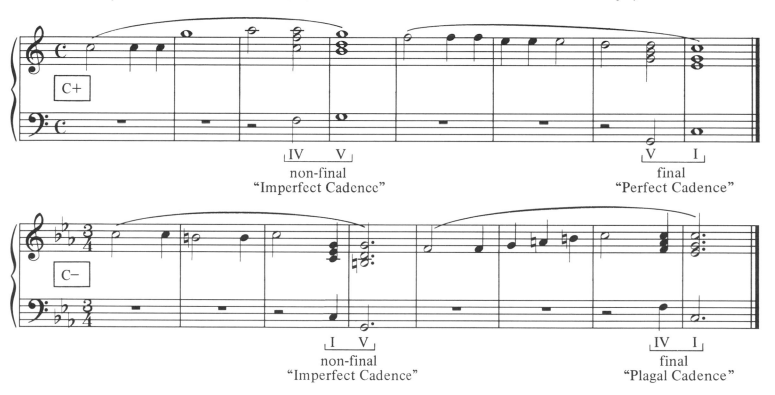

IV V	V I
non-final	final
"Imperfect Cadence"	"Perfect Cadence"

I V	IV I
non-final	final
"Imperfect Cadence"	"Plagal Cadence"

I II

PERFECT CADENCES

Perfect Cadences in Keyboard Style

The term *keyboard style* is used to refer to cadences and other chord progressions in which all three notes of each triad are played in close position with the right hand, and only the bass note is played with the left hand. The following examples in keyboard style illustrate the melodic progressions most commonly found in Perfect Cadences. Notice that in these examples the melody ends on the tonic note (1).

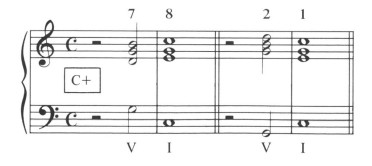

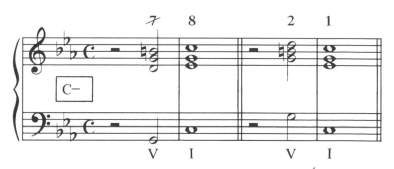

The following examples illustrate the other melodic progressions found in Perfect Cadences. In these progressions, the melody ends on the mediant (3) or dominant (5) of the key.

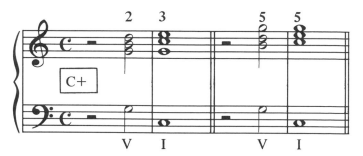 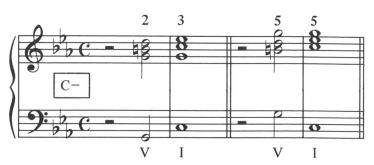

In Perfect Cadences in keyboard style, the root of each triad is *always* placed in the bass staff (left hand). The root, third and fifth of each triad are found in the treble staff (right hand), in *close* position, and the two chords are connected as smoothly as possible. The position of the two lower notes in each right-hand chord is determined by the melody note. If the root of a triad is in the melody, the fifth and the third are beneath it, in *that* order. If the third of a triad is in the melody, the root and the fifth are beneath it, in *that* order. If the fifth of a triad is in the melody, the third and the root are beneath it, in *that* order. The right-hand triad thus remains in close position.

A Perfect Cadence usually involves two measures of music. In most cases, the tonic chord occurs on the first beat of the last measure, while the dominant chord occurs immediately before it in the preceding measure.

A Perfect Cadence may occur in any major or minor key. In minor keys, the leading note of the dominant chord is always raised by means of an accidental. The bass note of the dominant chord can approach the tonic from above or below.

Writing Perfect Cadences in Keyboard Style

When asked to write a Perfect Cadence in a given key and time signature (e.g., "Write a two-bar Perfect Cadence in F minor in $\frac{4}{4}$ time"), you should:

1) Write the correct key signature and time signature.

2) Write the left-hand part. (This will consist of the dominant note followed by the tonic note of the key. The tonic note should be placed on the first beat of the last measure. The dominant note should be on an appropriate beat of the second-last measure. Study the cadences in question 1 of the following exercises as examples.)

3) Symbolize the chord progression for the Perfect Cadence (V–I) beneath the left-hand part.

4) List the notes of the dominant chord (c, e♮, g) and the tonic chord (f, a♭, c) beneath the chord symbols.

5) Choose an appropriate melody for the cadence (e.g., 7–8 or 2-1) and write it on the treble staff. (In the key of F minor, the 7–8 melody would be notes E to F, and the 2-1 melody would be notes G to F.)

6) On the treble staff, beneath the melody, add the two notes that complete each right-hand triad. Use close position.

7) Add any rests necessary to complete the time of the bars in which the cadence is written. *Since the given example is in a minor key, the leading note will require an accidental.*

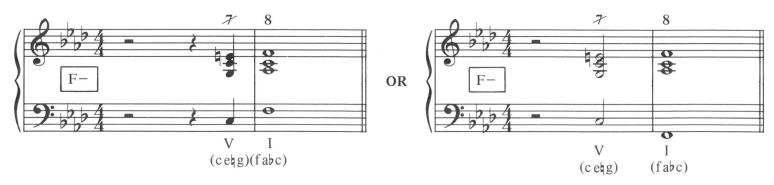

I II EXERCISES ON PERFECT CADENCES

1. For each of the following Perfect Cadences:
   (i) name the key;
   (ii) symbolize each chord;
   (iii) name the notes of each chord;
   (iv) add the Arabic numerals for the melody notes;
   (v) play the cadence.

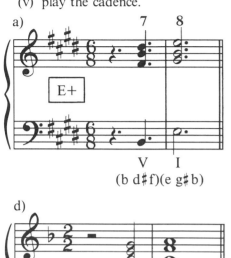

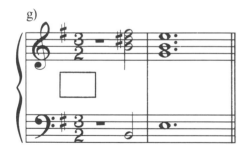  

38

2. For each of the following examples:
   (i) add the key signature;
   (ii) write a Perfect Cadence in the given key;
  (iii) play the cadence.

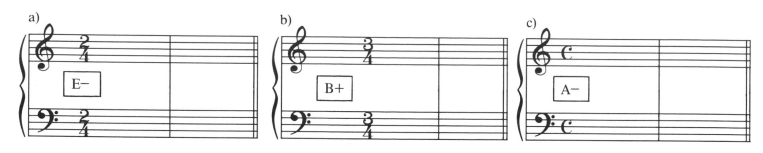

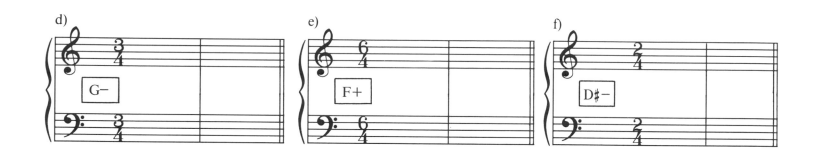

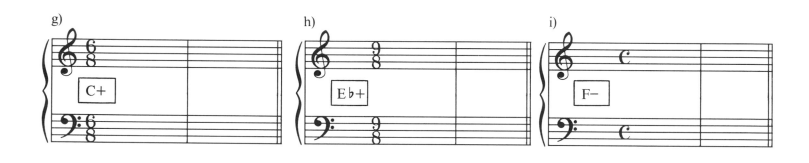

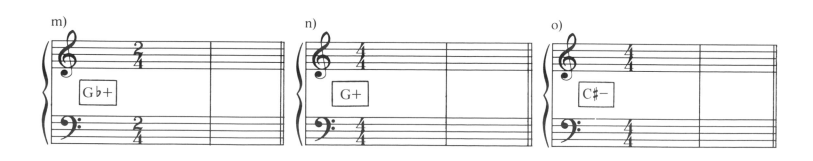

I II

PLAGAL CADENCES

Plagal Cadences in Keyboard Style

As stated earlier, the *Plagal Cadence* consists of the chord progression IV–I. The following examples of Plagal Cadences can exist in any major or minor key. The three possible melodic progressions for Plagal Cadences are tonic–tonic (1-1), subdominant–mediant (4-3), and submediant–dominant (6-5).

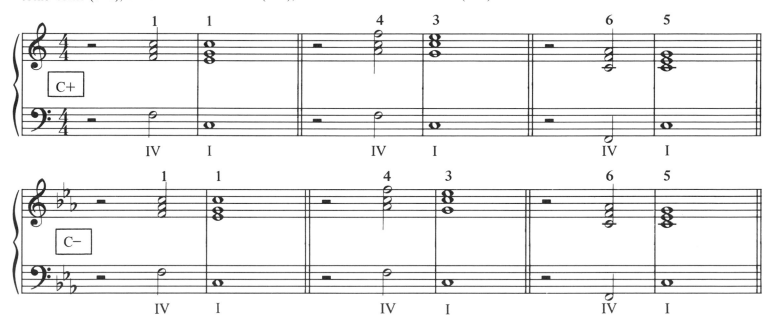

In Plagal Cadences, the root of each triad is always placed in the bass. The root, third and fifth of each triad are found in the treble staff (right hand), in *close* position, and the two chords are connected as smoothly as possible.

A Plagal Cadence usually involves two measures of music. In most cases, the tonic chord occurs on the first beat of the last measure, while the subdominant chord occurs immediately before it in the preceding measure.

The bass of the subdominant chord can approach the tonic from above or below.

Writing Plagal Cadences in Keyboard Style

When asked to write a Plagal Cadence in a given key and time signature (e.g., "Write a two-bar Plagal Cadence in C♯ minor in 𝄴 time"), you should:

1) Write the correct key signature and time signature.

2) Write the left-hand part. (This will consist of the subdominant note followed by the tonic note of the key. The tonic note should be placed on the first beat of the last measure. The subdominant note should be on an appropriate beat of the second-last measure. Study the cadences in question 1 of the following exercises as examples.)

3) Symbolize the chord progression for the Plagal Cadence (IV–I) beneath the left-hand part.

4) List the notes of the subdominant chord (f♯, a, c♯) and the tonic chord (c♯, e, g♯) beneath the chord symbols.

5) Choose an appropriate melody for the cadence (e.g., 1-1, 4-3, or 6-5) and write it on the treble staff.

6) On the treble staff, beneath the melody, add the two notes that complete each right-hand triad. Use close position.

7) Add any rests necessary to complete the time of the bars in which the cadence is written.

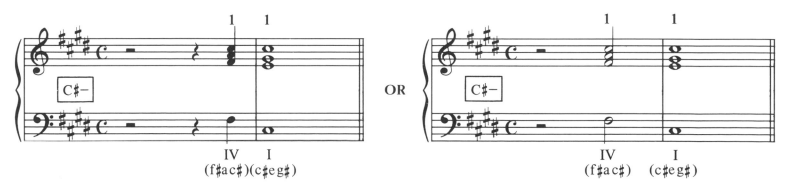

I II | EXERCISES ON PLAGAL CADENCES |

1. For each of the following Plagal Cadences:
  (i) name the key;
  (ii) symbolize each chord;
  (iii) name the notes of each chord;
  (iv) add the Arabic numerals for the melody notes;
  (v) play the cadence.

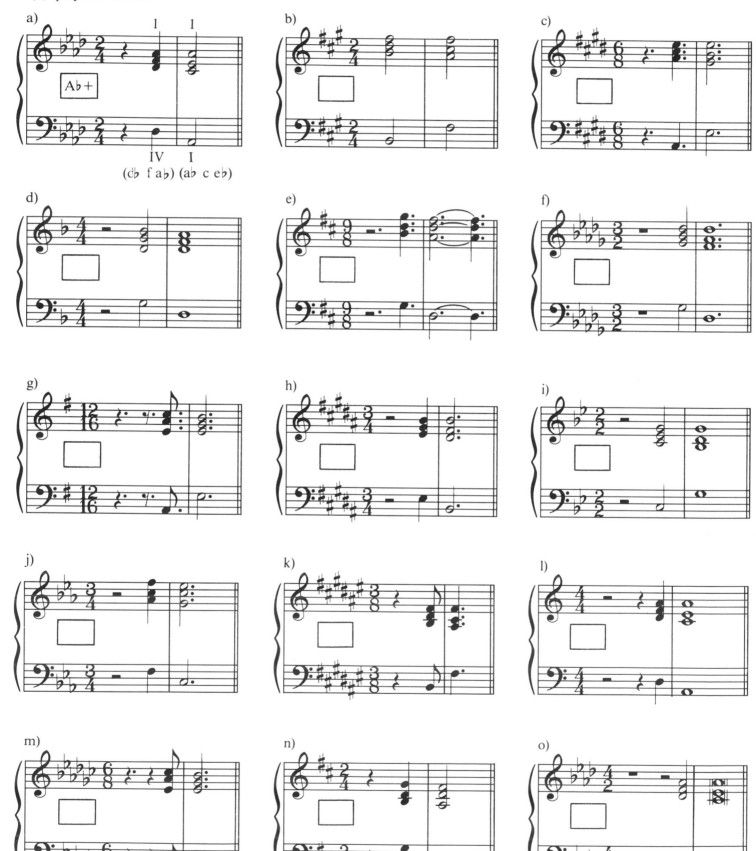

2. For each of the following examples:
- (i) add the key signature;
- (ii) write a Plagal Cadence in the given key;
- (iii) play the cadence.

a)

b)

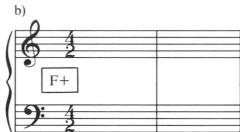

c)

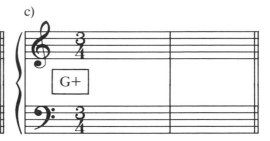

d)

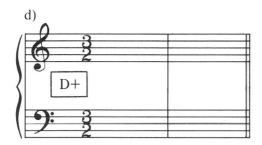

e)

f)

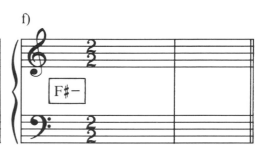

g)

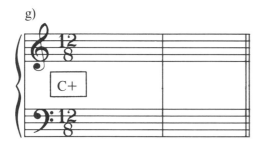

h)

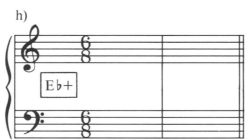

i)

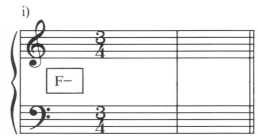

j)

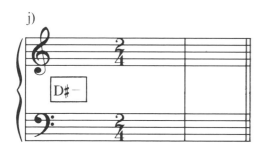

k)

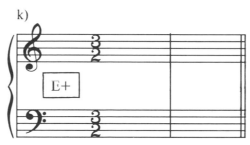

l)

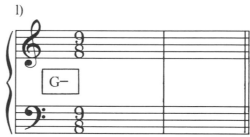

m)

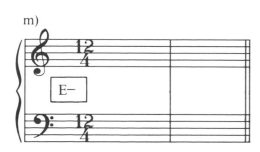

n)

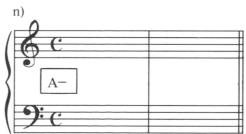

o)

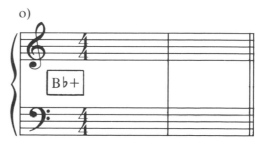

3. The following thematic excerpts contain Perfect or Plagal cadences, not necessarily in keyboard style. For each excerpt:

  (i) name the key;

 (ii) symbolize the chords of the cadence;

(iii) name the cadence;

(iv) play the excerpt.

Harpsichord Concerto No. 5, 3rd mvt.

We Three Kings of Orient Are

Requiem

The Wild Rider, Op. 68, No. 8

Violin Concerto No. 2, 3rd mvt.

II

IMPERFECT CADENCES

Imperfect Cadences in Keyboard Style

A non-final cadence punctuates a musical phrase in much the same way as a comma punctuates a literary phrase. The *phrase* is ended but the *sentence* is not yet complete. In music, this non-final effect is achieved by placing a dominant chord at the end of a phrase.

The chord progressions I–V, II–V, IV–V, and VI–V all form *Imperfect Cadences* when placed at the end of a phrase. We shall concentrate on the progressions I–V and IV–V.

In the I–V cadence, the bass (left-hand) part moves from tonic to dominant. The treble (right-hand) part includes all three notes of each triad, and the two chords are connected as smoothly as possible. The following examples illustrate the most common melodic patterns for the I–V cadence.

In the IV–V cadence, the left-hand part moves up a major 2nd, from the subdominant to the dominant. The right-hand part includes all three notes of each triad, and the two chords are connected as smoothly as possible. Notice that the three right-hand notes always *descend* in contrary motion to the ascending left-hand part. The following examples illustrate the most common melodic patterns for the IV–V cadence.

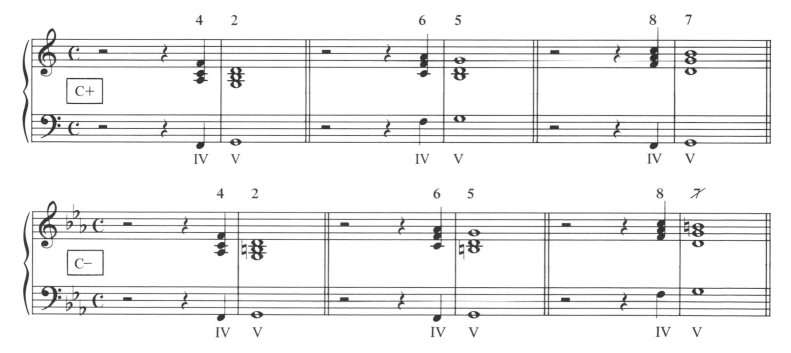

44

1. For each of the following Imperfect Cadences:
  (i) name the key;
 (ii) symbolize the chords;
(iii) name the notes of each chord;
(iv) add the Arabic numerals for the melody notes;
 (v) play the cadence.

2. For each of the following examples:
   (i) name the key;
   (ii) symbolize the chords;
   (iii) name the notes of each chord;
   (iv) complete the Imperfect Cadence above the given bass, then add the Arabic numerals for your melody;
   (v) play the cadence.

3. For each of the following excerpts:
  (i) name the key;
  (ii) symbolize the chords of the cadence;
  (iii) name the cadence;
  (iv) play the excerpt.

Valses Nobles, Op. 77

F. Schubert

Piano Sonata No. 4, 3rd mvt.

L. van Beethoven

Liederkreis, Op. 24, No. 8

R. Schumann

Symphony No. 3, 3rd mvt.

L. van Beethoven

The Indian Queen

H. Purcell

II

CADENCES AT THE ENDS OF MELODIC PHRASES

Writing Cadences at the Ends of Melodic Phrases

You may be asked to write cadences at the ends of given melodic phrases. For example, a question may state, "Write an appropriate cadence at the end of each four-bar phrase in the following melody. Symbolize the chords of the cadences and classify the cadences as Imperfect, Perfect or Plagal."

The steps to follow in answering this question are:

1) Name the key.

2) Play the melody.

3) Mark the Arabic numerals above the last two notes of each phrase.

For the final cadence:

1) Determine from the melodic progression if the cadence is Perfect or Plagal.

2) Symbolize the chords as V–I or IV–I.

3) Write the left-hand notes (the root of each chord) in thc bass staff.

4) Complete the triads in the right-hand part *beneath* the given melody.

5) Add any rests necessary to complete the time of the bars in which the cadence is written.

6) Name the cadence.

For the first cadence:

1) Determine from the melodic progression if the Imperfect Cadence should be IV–V or I–V. (Remember that the melodic pattern 8-7 can accommodate either progression.) Only rarely is the cadence at this point Perfect or Plagal.

2) Symbolize the chords.

3) Write the left-hand notes (the root of each chord) in the bass staff.

4) Complete the triads in the right-hand part *beneath* the given melody.

5) Add any rests necessary to complete the time of the bars in which the cadence is written.

6) Name the cadence.

48

EXERCISES ON CADENTIAL HARMONY

1. For each of the following examples:
(i) name the key;
(ii) play the example;
(iii) add the Arabic numerals for the melody notes of the cadence;
(iv) symbolize each cadential chord;
(v) name the cadence.

a)

b)

c)

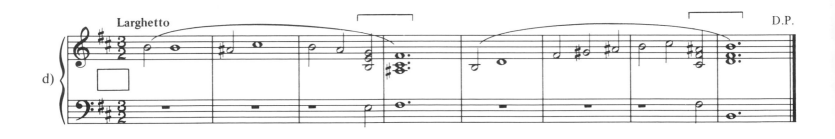

d)

e)

49

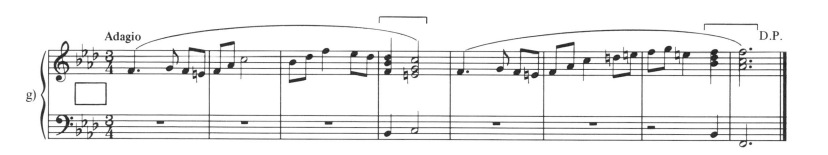

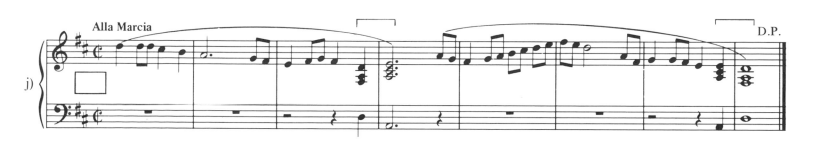

2. For each of the following melodies:
   (i)   name the key;
   (ii) sing the melody;
   (iii) add the Arabic numerals for the melody notes of the cadence;
   (iv) write an appropriate cadence under the bracket at the end of each 4-bar phrase, and symbolize the cadential chords;
   (v)   name the cadences;
   (vi) play the melody with the cadences you have written.

Dance

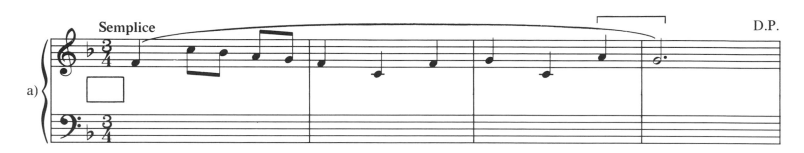

a)

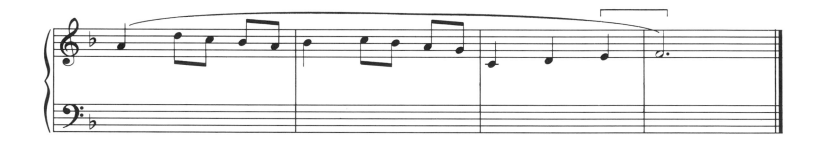

Maestoso

b)

Fanfare

52

Gigue

Funeral March

Polonaise

3. THE EXPANSION AND EXTENSION OF TRIADS

Sarabande

George Frideric Handel
(1685-1759)

George Frideric Handel composed the opening section of his well-known "Sarabande" for harpsichord in an essentially four-part texture. This texture is created through the use of *expanded* and *extended* triads.

A triad is *expanded* when one or more of its notes are repeated, or doubled, in another octave. In measure 1, the triad of D minor (D, F, A) is expanded by repeating the root, D. This doubling creates a *four-note chord*.

A triad is *extended* when a new note is added a 7th above the root. This is the case on beat 2 of measure 13, where a C major triad is extended to a *dominant seventh chord* (C, E, G, B♭), here in first inversion.

II

THE EXPANSION OF TRIADS

Triads in Four-Note Form

A four-note chord can be created by doubling one of the notes of a triad. To double in close position, take the lowest note of the close position triad and write it an octave higher. For example:

To analyse a chord of four notes, determine the *root* of the triad on which the four-note form is based, the *type* of triad (major, minor, augmented, or diminished), and whether the chord is in root position, first inversion, or second inversion.

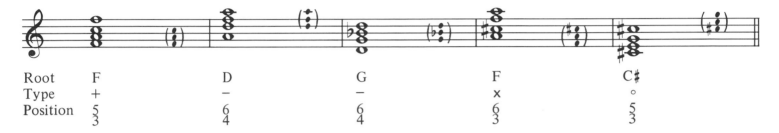

Root	F		D		G		F		C♯
Type	+		−		−		x		°
Position	5⁄3		6⁄4		6⁄4		6⁄3		5⁄3

Four-Note Forms in Close and Open Position

A triad in four-note form is in close position when the notes are written as closely together as possible, the intervals between adjacent notes being either 3rds or 4ths. When a four-note form is in close position, it is contained within the range of an octave.

A triad in four-note form is in open position when the notes are *not* written as closely together as possible. In open position, the notes will not be contained within the range of an octave. The following chords are all in open position.

To analyse an open position triad in four-note form, eliminate the doubled note and write the three notes of the triad in root and close position. Determine the root and type of the triad. If the root of the triad is the lowest note of the given four-note form, the chord is in root position. If the third of the triad is the lowest note, the chord is in first inversion. If the fifth of the triad is the lowest note, the chord is in second inversion.

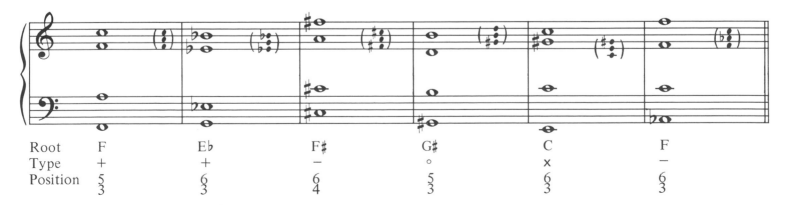

Root	F		E♭		F♯		G♯		C		F
Type	+		+		−		°		x		−
Position	5⁄3		6⁄3		6⁄4		5⁄3		6⁄3		6⁄3

Four-Part Song

Sing (or sing and play) this four-part folk-song setting as an introduction to the sound of a piece containing close and open position triads in four-note form.

O Sanctissima

arr. David Paul

D+   O   sanc - tis - si - ma____   O   pi - is - si - ma____

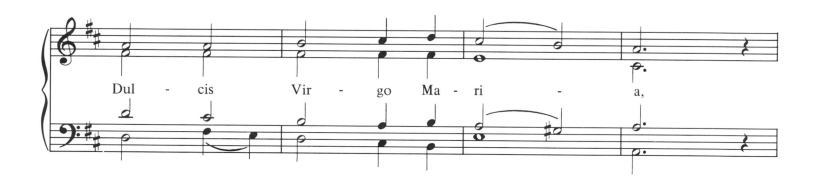

Dul - cis   Vir - go   Ma - ri - a,

Ma - ter   a - ma - ta,   in - te - me - ra - ta,

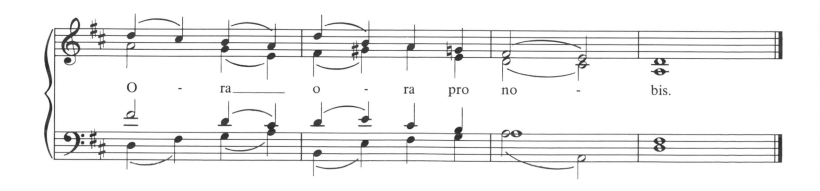

O - ra____   o - ra   pro   no - bis.

The Further Expansion of Triads

You have just seen that a triad in four-note form is built by doubling one note of the triad. Through doubling, it is also possible to build chords of five, six, seven and eight or more notes. No matter how many notes a chord contains, if by stripping away the doublings you are left with only a triad, the chord is simply an expansion of that triad. Here are some examples:

Root	C	F#	G	D
Type	+	°	–	x
Position	$\frac{5}{3}$	$\frac{6}{3}$	$\frac{6}{3}$	$\frac{5}{3}$

R. Wagner

Root	Db		Gb	Db	Ab	Db
Type	+		+	+	+	+
Position	$\frac{5}{3}$		$\frac{5}{3}$	$\frac{5}{3}$	$\frac{5}{3}$	$\frac{5}{3}$

Traditional Chord Symbols

In Chapter 1 you learned that traditional chord symbols can be used to symbolize diatonic triads (triads containing only notes from a given major or minor scale). The same system is used to symbolize chords based on expansions of these triads. A Roman numeral is used to designate the scale degree of the root of each chord, and Arabic numerals ($\frac{5}{3}$, $\frac{6}{3}$, $\frac{6}{4}$) indicate whether the chord is in root position, first inversion, or second inversion. Root position chords are so common that the Arabic numerals are generally omitted when symbolizing them. In the case of first inversion chords, $\frac{6}{3}$ is usually abbreviated to 6.

D.P.

I   III   IV   V   II   I$^6_4$ V   VI   II^6 V   III^6 I

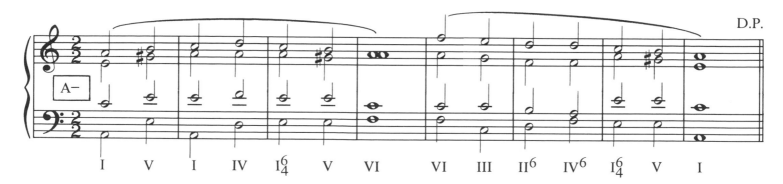

<blockquote>
D.P.
</blockquote>

I   V   I   IV   I⁶₄   V   VI   VI   III   II⁶   IV⁶   I⁶₄   V   I

O ⟮ *Popular Chord Symbols* ⟯

Popular chord symbols work in the same way for four-note forms of triads as they do for triads. The chord is designated by a symbol indicating its root and quality. The symbol **D**, for example, indicates a major chord with root D. The symbol **F♯m** indicates a minor chord with root F♯. If the chord symbol is followed by a slash and another capital letter, the bass note will be a note other than the root (usually the third or fifth of the triad). The symbol **G/D**, for example, stands for a G major triad with D in the bass.

Remember that triads in four-note form include one doubled note, often the root, and that the three upper notes of the chord may be arranged in many different ways.

Play the following excerpt from a four-part setting of the song "O Sanctissima". Notice that popular chord symbols have been placed above the score. These symbols correspond to the chords that appear directly underneath.

O Sanctissima

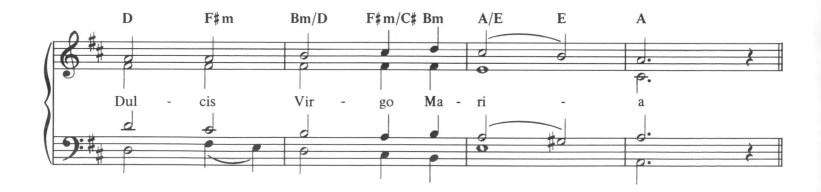

II EXERCISES ON CHORDS

1. Analyse the following close position chords.

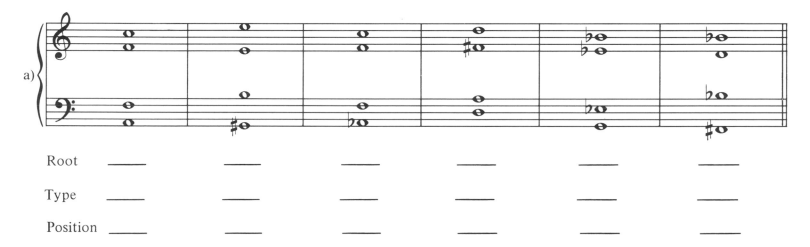

Root   _____   _____   _____   _____   _____   _____   _____   _____

Type   _____   _____   _____   _____   _____   _____   _____   _____

Position _____   _____   _____   _____   _____   _____   _____   _____

2. Analyse the following open position chords.

a)

Root   _____   _____   _____   _____   _____   _____

Type   _____   _____   _____   _____   _____   _____

Position _____   _____   _____   _____   _____   _____

b)

Root   _____   _____   _____   _____   _____   _____

Type   _____   _____   _____   _____   _____   _____

Position _____   _____   _____   _____   _____   _____

II EXERCISES ON CHORDAL TEXTURES

1. Analyse each boxed solid or broken chord in the following composition by specifying its root, quality and position. Play this piece on the piano.

Larghetto, Op. 30, No. 17

Mauro Giuliani
(1781-1829)

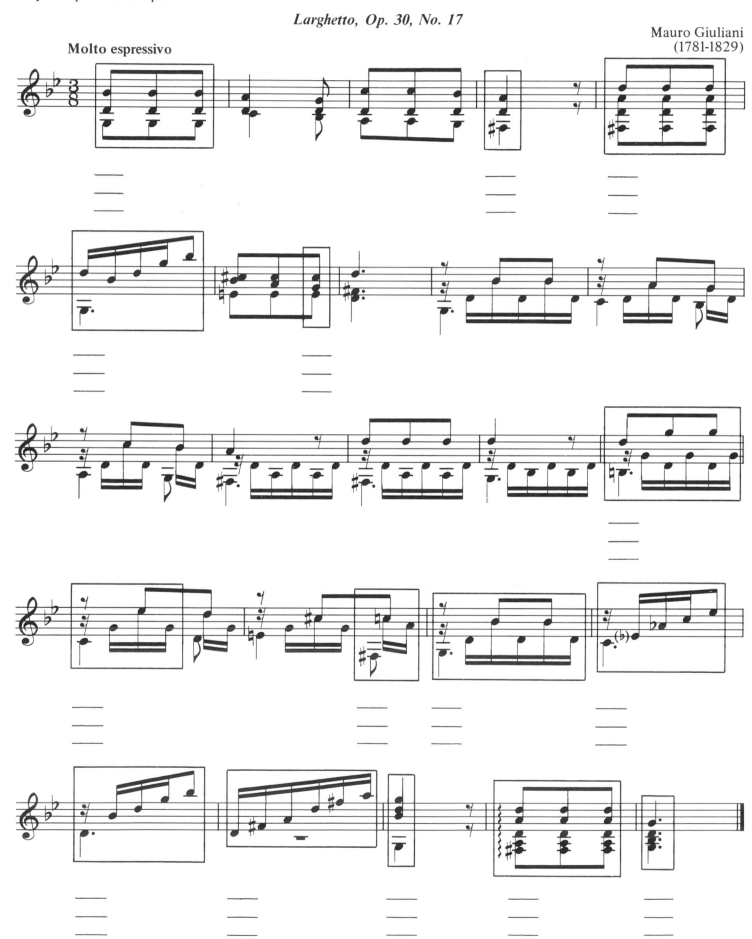

2. For each of the following thematic excerpts:
   (i) analyse the chords by specifying the root, quality and position wherever lines are provided;
   (ii) play the excerpt.

Nocturne, Op. 37, No. 1

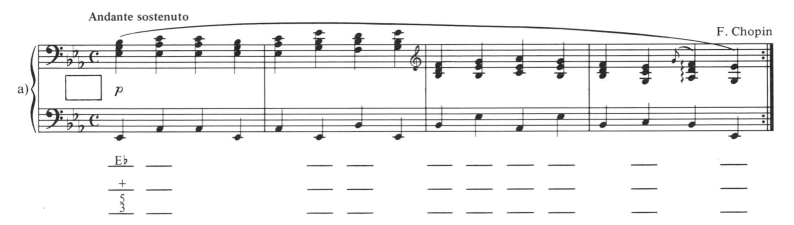

F. Chopin

Piano Sonata No. 9, 1st mvt.

L. van Beethoven

Overture to Cosi fan tutte

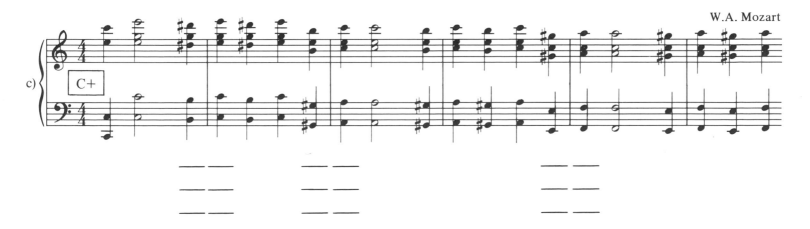

W.A. Mozart

3. For each of the following choral excerpts:
   (i) name the key;
   (ii) play the excerpt;
   (iii) write the traditional chord symbol beneath each chord.

The Creation

Messiah

Ave Maria

*Circled melodic notes in the examples shown above are non-harmonic notes and should not be taken into account when analysing the chords.

O EXERCISES ON POPULAR CHORD SYMBOLS

1. Add the popular chord symbols wherever lines are provided.

2. Mark the popular chord symbols wherever lines are provided in the following song.

All Through the Night

Calmato

Wales

Sleep my child and peace at-tend thee All through the night.
Guard - ian an - gels God will send thee All through the night.

Soft the drow-sy hours are creep-ing hill and vale in slum - ber steep-ing,

I my lov - ing vi - gil keep-ing, All through the night.

THE EXTENSION OF TRIADS

II

The Dominant Seventh

The *dominant seventh* is a chord of four different notes. To form this chord, the dominant triad of a key is extended by adding a *minor 7th* above the root (a minor 3rd above the fifth). The symbol for a dominant seventh chord is V7.

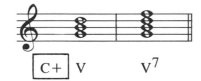
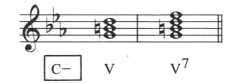

In the minor mode, the dominant seventh chord, being *harmony*, contains notes drawn from the *harmonic* minor scale. This includes scale degrees 5, 7̂, 2 and 4. The 7th degree appears in the raised form as a leading note. Thus the dominant seventh of a minor key contains exactly the same notes as the dominant seventh of its tonic major.

A dominant seventh chord can be constructed on *any* given note by writing a major 3rd, perfect 5th and minor 7th above it. For example, a dominant seventh on B♭ contains the notes B♭, D, F, and A♭.

The dominant seventh is in root position when the root is the lowest note, in first inversion when the third is the lowest note, in second inversion when the fifth is the lowest note, and in third inversion when the seventh is the lowest note. Study the following examples.

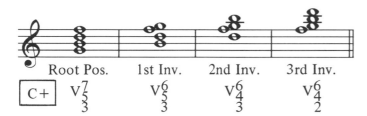
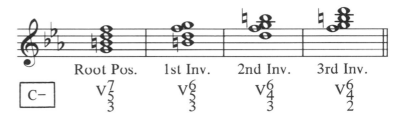

In the examples shown above, the Arabic numerals $\frac{7}{5}$, $\frac{6}{5}$, $\frac{6}{4}$ and $\frac{6}{4}$ symbolize the intervals that the upper three
notes of the chord form with the lowest note. These numerals are abbreviated as follows:

Dominant seventh in root position: V⁷   Dominant seventh in second inversion: V⁴₃

Dominant seventh in first inversion: V⁶₅   Dominant seventh in third inversion: V⁴₂

Dominant Sevenths in Close and Open Position

Like triads and their expansions, dominant sevenths can be written in open position. The three upper voices can occur in any order, because it is the bass note alone that determines whether the chord is in root position or inverted. Study these examples.

Close Position

Open Position

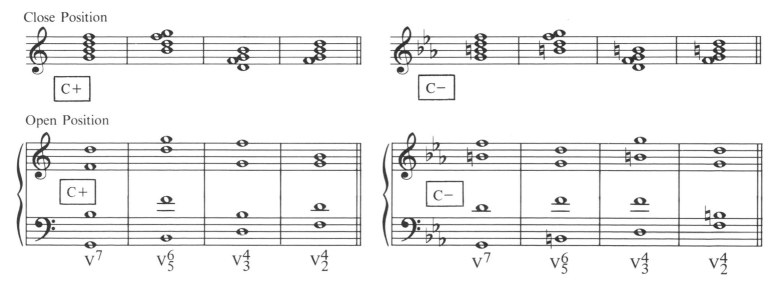

Dominant Seventh Song

The following is an excerpt of a song from Verdi's opera *Rigoletto*. Pay particular attention to the piano accompaniment, which consists of only two chords, the tonic (A♭, C, E♭) and the dominant seventh (E♭, G, B♭, D♭).*

Act I, No. 2 from Rigoletto

Giuseppe Verdi
(1813-1901)

*In dominant seventh chords, the fifth is occasionally omitted and the root doubled (e.g., E♭, G, D♭, E♭).

O **Popular Chord Symbols for Dominant Sevenths**

In the system of popular chord symbols, a dominant seventh chord is symbolized by means of a capital letter followed by the numeral **7**.

D7 symbolizes the V7 of G+ or G– (D, F♯, A, C).

E♭7 symbolizes the V7 of A♭+ or A♭– (E♭, G, B♭, D♭).

F♯7 symbolizes the V7 of B+ or B– (F♯, A♯, C♯, E).

If any note *other* than the root of the chord is to be played as the lowest, this note is indicated by a second capital letter preceded by a slash.

D7/A symbolizes V$^4_3$ of G+ or G– (D, F♯, A, C with bass note A).

E♭7/D♭ symbolizes V$^4_2$ of A♭+ or A♭– (E♭, G, B♭, D♭ with bass note D♭).

F7/A symbolizes V$^6_5$ of B♭+ or B♭– (F, A, C, E♭ with bass note A).

Here are some popular chord symbols and their realizations in both close and open positions.

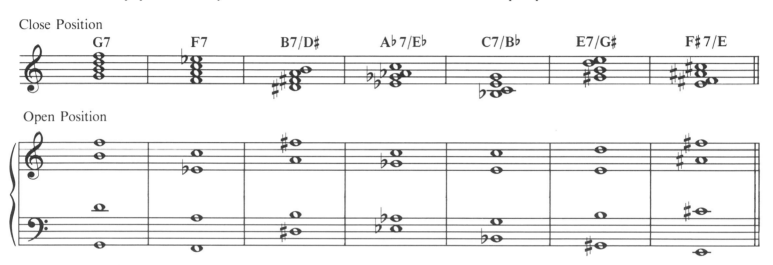

O **Secondary Dominant Sevenths**

The dominant seventh chord can be created diatonically *only* on the dominant of a major or harmonic minor scale. Building a seventh chord on any *other* degree of these scales will not produce the dominant seventh sound (i.e., a major triad extended by a minor 3rd above its fifth). Nonetheless, the dominant seventh sound can be created on these other degrees by the addition of accidentals. These accidentals yield chromatic notes (notes not from the scale), and the resulting chromatically-altered chords are called *secondary dominant sevenths*.

The following excerpt from a song by Franz Schubert, "Der Entfernten", contains three secondary dominant seventh chords. Each is enclosed within a box.

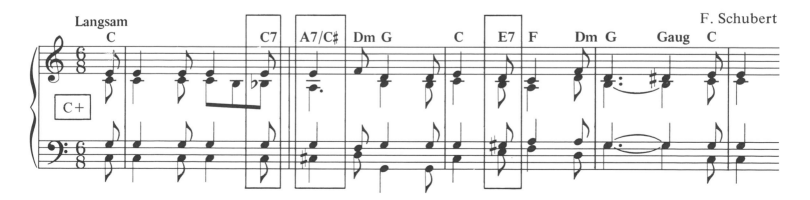

II EXERCISES ON DOMINANT SEVENTHS

1. For each of the following examples:
   (i) add the key signature;
   (ii) write a close position dominant seventh chord in root position.

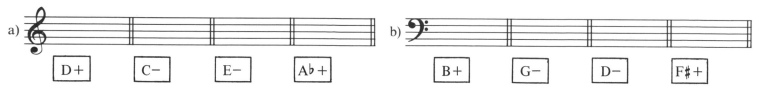

2. For each of the following examples:
   (i) add the key signature of the *major* key;
   (ii) name the key;
   (iii) write a root position dominant seventh chord above the given note;
   (iv) write the three inversions of this dominant seventh chord.

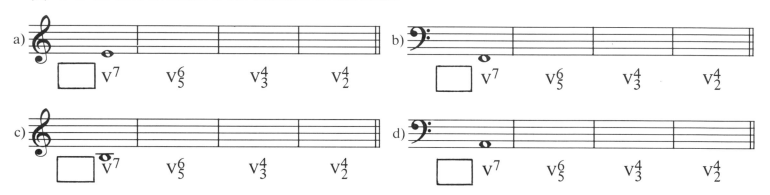

3. For each of the following close position dominant seventh chords:
   (i) name the key;
   (ii) state the root;
   (iii) specify the position.

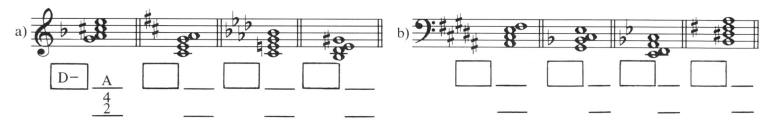

4. For each of the following open position dominant seventh chords:
   (i) name the key;
   (ii) state the root;
   (iii) specify the position.

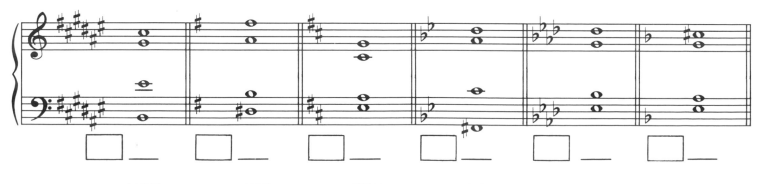

5. For each of the following chords:
   (i) create a dominant seventh by adding accidentals;
   (ii) name the *major* key in which the chord is found;
   (iii) specify the position.

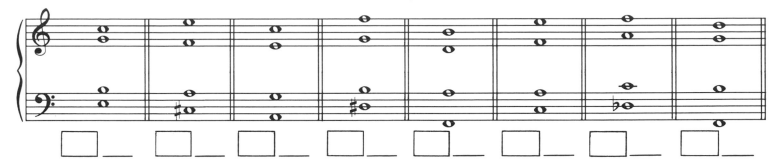

6. For each of the following chords:
   (i) create the dominant seventh of a *minor* key by adding a key signature and any necessary accidentals;
   (ii) name the *minor* key in which the chord is found;
   (iii) specify the position.

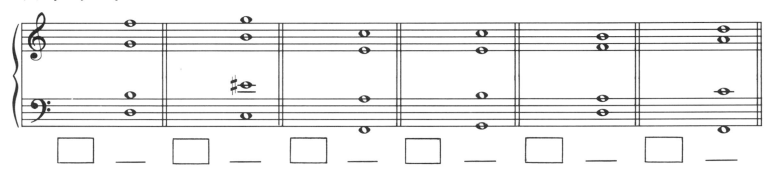

II | EXERCISES ON CHORDAL TEXTURES |

1. For each of the following thematic excerpts:
   (i) name the key;
   (ii) put a box around any dominant seventh chords;
   (iii) specify the root and position of each dominant seventh.

Symphony No. 5, 4th mvt.

L. van Beethoven

Clarinet Quintet, 1st mvt.

W.A. Mozart

Lohengrin

R. Wagner

Con moto moderato

c)

Symphony in D Minor, 2nd mvt.

C. Franck

Allegretto

d)

p

Piano Sonata No. 15, 3rd mvt.

L. van Beethoven

Allegro vivace

e)

p

A+

Piano Concerto No. 1, 1st mvt.

L. van Beethoven

Allegro con brio

f)

Piano Sonata No. 23, 2nd mvt.

L. van Beethoven

Andante con moto

g)

p *cresc.* *p*

V_5^6

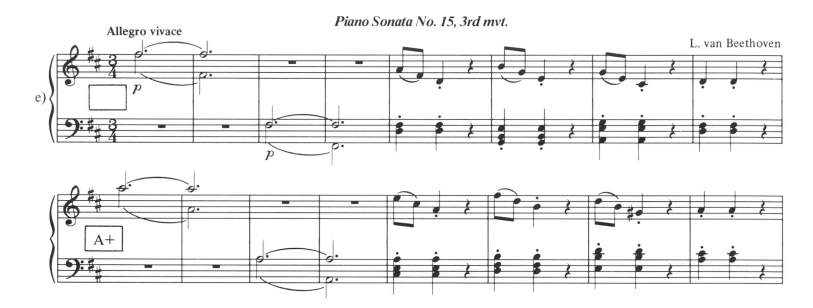

O | EXERCISES ON POPULAR CHORD SYMBOLS |

1. Add the popular chord symbols wherever lines are provided.

The Poor Orphan Child, Op. 68, No. 6

Symphony No. 1, 1st mvt.

Piano Sonata No. 21, 1st mvt.

Symphonic Etude, Op. 13, No. 9

Presto possibile

R. Schumann

Scheherazade

Allegro non troppo

N. Rimsky-Korsakov

Waltz, Op. 39, No. 2

Andante sostenuto

J. Brahms

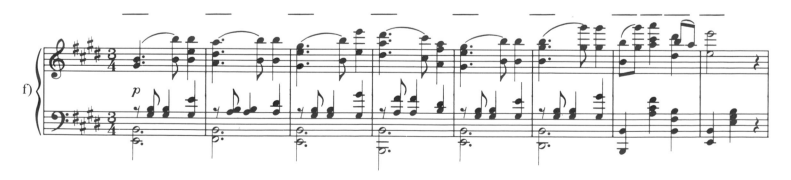

2. Perform the following composition on the piano. Play the melody with the right hand and the chords designated by popular chord symbols with the left hand.

Waltz, Op. 39, No. 15

J. Brahms

O

OTHER SEVENTH CHORDS

The *diminished seventh chord* is an extension of the diminished triad. It is formed by adding a *diminished 7th* above the root (a minor 3rd above the fifth). The following are all root position diminished seventh chords. Each is written first in close position and then in one of the many possible open position spacings.

Close Position

Open Position

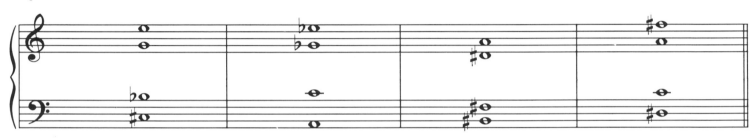

Like all other chords, the diminished seventh can be inverted. If the third is the lowest note, the chord is in first inversion. If the fifth is the lowest note, the chord is in second inversion. If the seventh is the lowest note, the chord is in third inversion.

Close Position

| Root
Position | 1st
Inversion | 2nd
Inversion | 3rd
Inversion |

Open Position

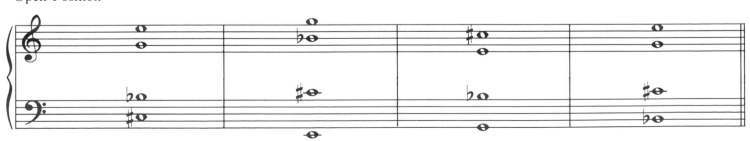

The popular chord symbol for the diminished seventh includes the figure **7** following the symbol for the diminished triad (e.g., **C♯dim7**, or **C♯°7**). The three inversions are indicated by the further addition of a slash and a capital letter representing the lowest note of the inversion. In the following examples, **C♯°7/E** indicates first inversion, **C♯°7/G** indicates second inversion, and **C♯°7/B♭** indicates third inversion.

Close Position

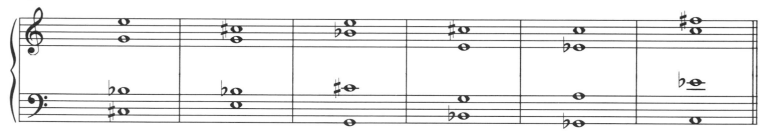

Open Position

Observe Schumann's use of diminished seventh chords in the following example.

R. Schumann

The Minor Seventh

The *minor seventh chord* is an extension of the minor triad. It is formed by adding a *minor 7th* above the root (a minor 3rd above the fifth). The following are all root position minor seventh chords. Each is written first in close position and then in one of the many possible open position spacings.

Close Position

Open Position

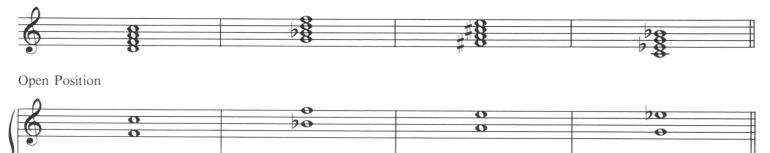

Like all other chords, the minor seventh can be inverted. Study the following example of a root position minor seventh chord followed by its three inversions.

Close Position

| Root Position | 1st Inversion | 2nd Inversion | 3rd Inversion |

Open Position

The minor seventh chord occasionally appears with its fifth lowered a semitone. In this case it is referred to as a "minor seventh-flat five" chord. Study these examples.

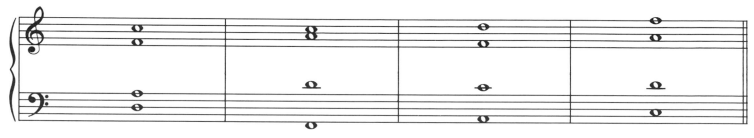

| Root Position | 1st Inversion | 2nd Inversion | 3rd Inversion | Root Position | Root Position | Root Position | Root Position |

The popular chord symbol for the minor seventh includes the figure **7** following the symbol for the minor triad (e.g., **Dm7**). The three inversions are indicated by the further addition of a slash and a capital letter representing the lowest note of the inversion. In the following examples, **Dm7/F** indicates first inversion, **Dm7/A** indicates second inversion, and **Dm7/C** indicates third inversion. The "minor seventh-flat five" chord adds the figure ♭5 beneath the figure **7** (e.g., **Dm♭$\frac{7}{5}$**). Study these examples.

Close Position

$$\text{Dm7} \quad \text{Dm7/F} \quad \text{Dm7/A} \quad \text{Dm7/C} \quad \text{Dm}♭\tfrac{7}{5}\text{/F} \quad \text{Fm7/A}♭ \quad \text{C}♯\text{m}♭\tfrac{7}{5}\text{/G} \quad \text{Am}♭\tfrac{7}{5}\text{/G}$$

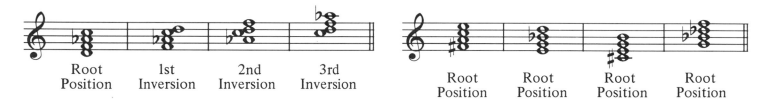

Open Position

Observe the use of two minor seventh chords in the following example.

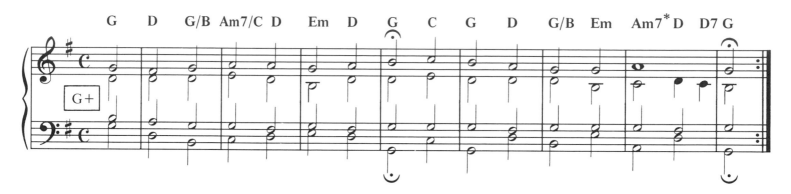

The Major Seventh

The *major seventh chord* is an extension of the major triad. It is formed by adding a *major 7th* above the root (a major 3rd above the fifth). The following are all root position major seventh chords. Each is written first in close position and then in one of the many possible open position spacings.

Close Position

Open Position

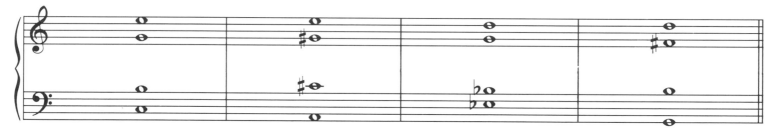

Like all other chords, the major seventh can be inverted. Study the following example of a root position major seventh chord followed by its three inversions.

Close Position

Root
Position

1st
Inversion

2nd
Inversion

3rd
Inversion

Open Position

*In the minor seventh chord, as in the dominant seventh, the fifth is occasionally omitted and the root doubled.

The popular chord symbol for the major seventh adds the figure **maj7** to the symbol for the major triad (e.g., **Cmaj7**). The inversions are indicated by the further addition of a slash and a capital letter representing the lowest note of the inversion. In the following examples, **Cmaj7/E** indicates first inversion, **Cmaj7/G** indicates second inversion, and **Cmaj7/B** indicates third inversion.

Close Position

Open Position

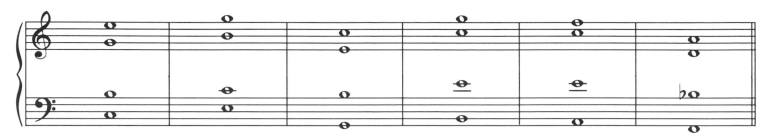

Observe J.S. Bach's use of a major seventh chord in the following example. (Non-harmonic notes are circled.)

J.S. Bach

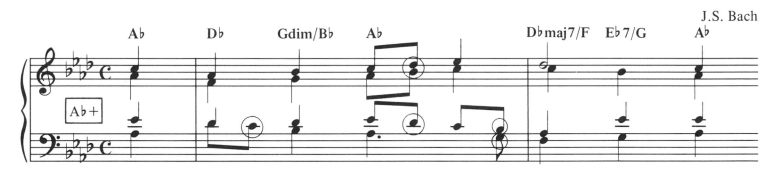

O   EXERCISES ON SEVENTH CHORDS AND POPULAR CHORD SYMBOLS

1. Write a diminished seventh chord in root position above each of the following notes.

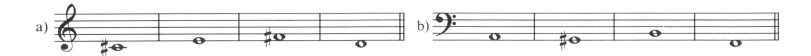

2. Write a minor seventh chord in root position above each of the following notes.

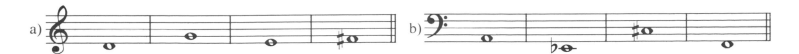

3. Write a major seventh chord in root position above each of the following notes.

4. Construct chords from the given popular chord symbols.

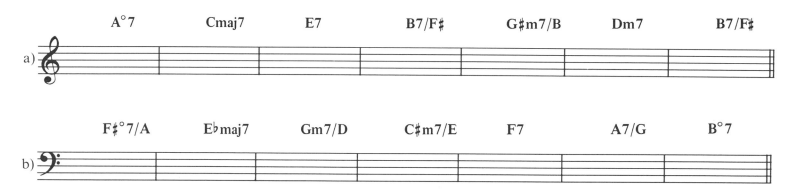

5. For each of the following thematic excerpts:
   (i) add the popular chord symbols wherever lines are provided;
   (ii) play the excerpt.

Prelude No. 1 from The Well-Tempered Clavier, Bk. I

Tyrle, tyrlow, tyrle, tyrlow

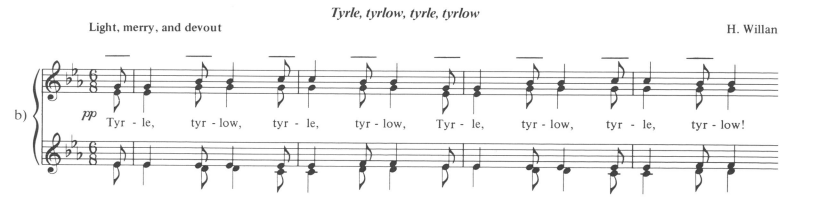

Piano Sonata No. 18, 1st mvt.

Allegro

L. van Beethoven

Symphony No. 3, 1st mvt.

Allegro con brio

J. Brahms

6. Perform the following compositions on the piano. Play the melody with the right hand and the chords designated by popular chord symbols with the left hand.

Melody in F

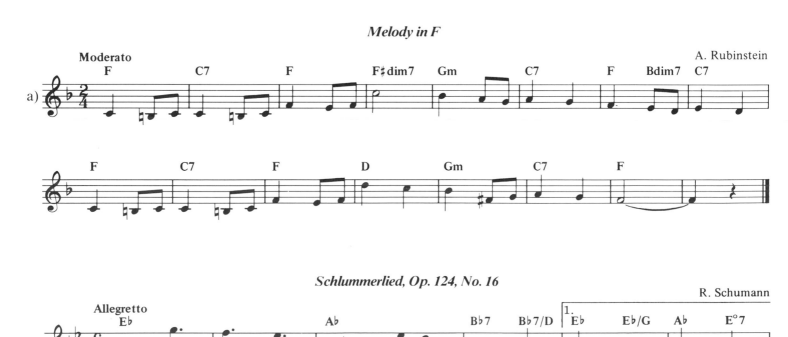

Moderato

A. Rubinstein

Schlummerlied, Op. 124, No. 16

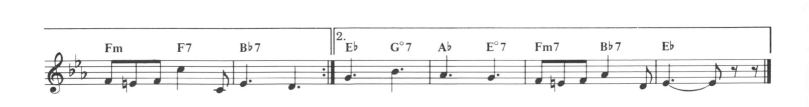

Allegretto

R. Schumann

Sarabande from Pour le piano

4. *FURTHER APPLICATIONS OF METER AND RHYTHM*

Promenade from Pictures at an Exhibition

Modest Mussorgsky
(1839-1881)

Mussorgsky's "Promenade", from *Pictures at an Exhibition,* introduces two concepts of meter that you have not yet encountered. First, almost every measure contains a change of time signature. Second, two of these signatures, $\frac{5}{4}$ and $\frac{7}{4}$, fall into the category of *hybrid meters.*

CHANGING TIME SIGNATURES

Changes of Time Signature

A composer may wish to change time signatures during the course of a composition. Changing time signatures occur frequently in music of the twentieth century. They are also an integral part of many folk songs.

Study the following Hungarian folk song as arranged for piano by Johannes Brahms. You will notice that although the time signature alternates regularly between ¾ and ⁴⁄₄, the quarter-note beat is constant from bar to bar.

If there is a regular alternation of time signatures from bar to bar within a piece, the composer may choose to indicate both time signatures at the beginning, as Brahms does in his folk-song setting. When you see two time signatures at the beginning of a piece, there will be a regular alternation of the two time signatures throughout the piece. If, on the other hand, a piece contains changing time signatures that do *not* alternate regularly, the composer first marks the time signature used at the beginning, and then indicates the new time signature whenever there is a change. *A time signature applies in the measure in which it appears and in every measure thereafter, until the appearance of a different time signature.*

Here is a folk song with a *regular* change of time signature.

Here is a folk song with an *irregular* change of time signature.

Song with Changing Time Signatures

To further acquaint yourself with the concept of music with changing time signatures, sing this setting of the Ojibway song, "My Bark Canoe". Notice that the time signature changes regularly from ¾ to ⁴⁄₄. This change, although regular, has been indicated in each bar to facilitate reading.

My Bark Canoe

arr. David Paul

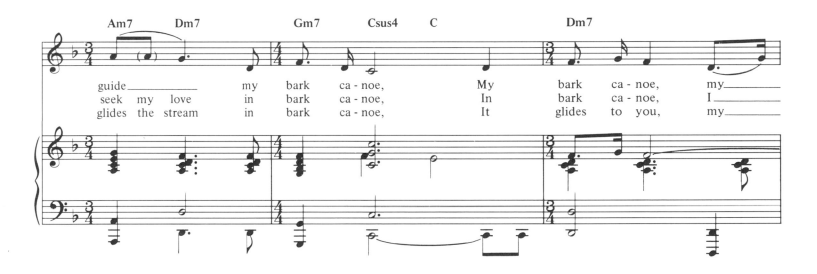

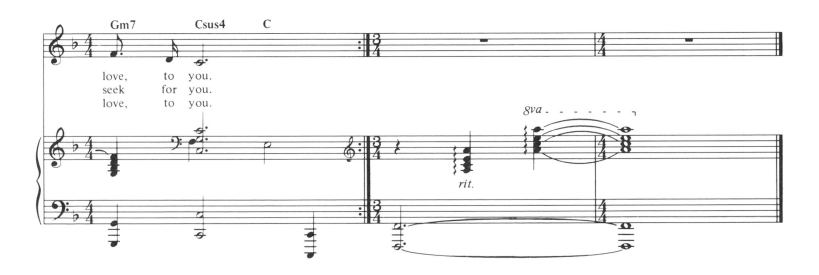

Alternating Simple and Compound Time

If a meter changes from simple to compound, or vice versa, either the *beat* or the *pulse* will remain constant. In each of the following examples, the time signature changes from $\frac{6}{8}$ to $\frac{2}{4}$. In Example 1, the *beat* remains constant. Therefore, the *dotted* quarter-note beat of the compound meter ($\frac{6}{8}$) must equal the *undotted* quarter-note beat of the simple meter ($\frac{2}{4}$). The indication ♩. = ♩ appears above the staff at the point where the meter changes.

Example 1

In Example 2, the *pulse* remains constant. This is indicated at the change of signature by ♪ = ♪ . Notice that when the signature changes from compound to simple time, the length of each beat is shortened by one eighth-note pulse.

Example 2

II EXERCISES ON CHANGING TIME SIGNATURES

1. For each of the following melodies:
   (i) add the time signatures;
   (ii) name the key;
   (iii) sing the melody.

88

2. For each of the following thematic excerpts:
  (i) add the time signatures;
  (ii) play the excerpt.

The Sacrifice from The Rite of Spring

Mysterious Circles of the Adolescents from The Rite of Spring

Ritual of the Ancestors from The Rite of Spring

Violin Sonata No. 1, 1st mvt.

Violin Concerto No. 2, 2nd mvt.

SYNCOPATION

Syncopation is a displacement of the regular pattern of beats in one or several bars of music, whereby a normally weak beat or weak part of a beat is stressed or emphasized. Placing a rest on a strong beat or an accent on a weak beat also produces syncopation.

Play the following theme from the fourth movement of Mozart's "Prague" Symphony. This theme illustrates syncopation produced by notes tied over the bar line. Notice that the strong—weak beat pattern of simple duple time is displaced by the rhythm Mozart has used. This displacement adds rhythmic excitement to the music.

W.A. Mozart

Piano Piece with Syncopation

Listen to a performance of Scott Joplin's "The Entertainer" to further acquaint yourself with the sound of music written in a syncopated style.

The Entertainer

Scott Joplin
(1868-1917)

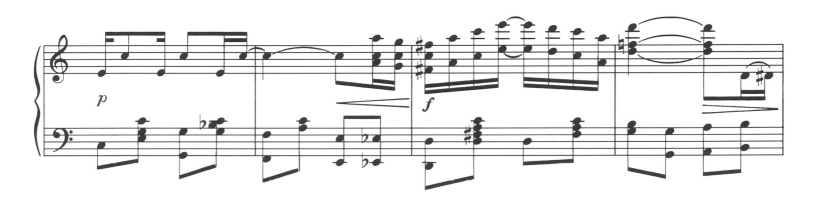

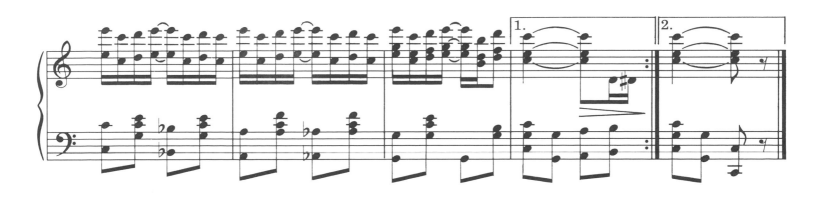

I II EXERCISES ON SYNCOPATION

1. For each of the following melodies:
   (i) name the key;
   (ii) clap the rhythm while counting the beats aloud;
   (iii) sing the melody.

2. For each of the following thematic excerpts:
   (i) name the key;
   (ii) add the time signature;
   (iii) clap the rhythm while counting the beats aloud;
   (iv) play the excerpt.

Valse, Op. 69, No. 2

Symphony No. 4, 4th mvt.

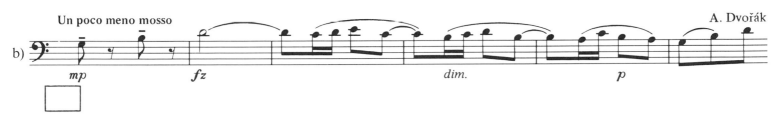

Water Music, 2nd Suite, 2nd mvt.

Piano Quintet, 1st mvt.

String Quartet, Op. 64, No. 3, 3rd mvt.

Elégie, Op. 3, No. 1

Symphony No. 9, 3rd mvt.

HYBRID METERS

In hybrid meters, some beats are dotted and some are not. In other words, a hybrid meter combines compound time and simple time. Like a simple or compound meter, a hybrid meter can be duple (two beats per measure), triple (three beats per measure), or quadruple (four beats per measure).

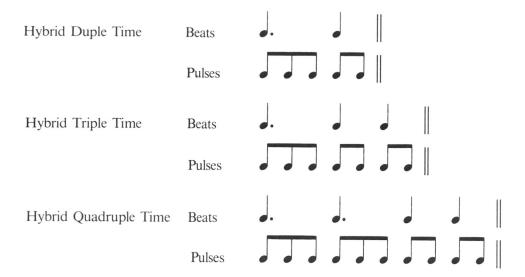

As in compound time signatures, the upper numeral of a hybrid time signature tells us how many *pulses* there are per bar, and the lower numeral tells us which type of note gets one pulse.

Hybrid Duple Time

In hybrid duple time there are two beats per bar, the first being stronger than the second. The first beat is usually a dotted note, consisting of three pulses, and the second beat is a simple note, consisting of two pulses. The upper numeral of the time signature is always 5 (indicating five pulses per bar), and the lower numeral is 2, 4, 8, or 16 (indicating the type of note that represents one pulse).

Chart of Hybrid Duple Time Signatures

Points to Remember:

1) Although there are five pulses per bar, these pulses form *two beats*.
2) Notes of eighth value or less (♪ , ♪ , ♪ , ♪) are beamed together if they belong to the same beat.
3) Since there is no *single* note equal to five pulses, a note sustained for an entire measure must be written as two notes joined by a tie.
4) Of the four time signatures shown above, $\frac{5}{4}$ and $\frac{5}{8}$ are the most frequently used.

In hybrid duple time, the first beat occasionally contains two pulses, while the second beat contains three pulses. When this occurs, the notes are grouped accordingly:

If the simple and compound beats do not follow one another in a regular sequence, the grouping of notes will always indicate which beat is simple and which is compound.

If a composition in hybrid duple time is performed slowly enough, its pulses begin to be felt as beats. In the example shown below, each bar has five beats rather than two, and the notes are grouped according to pulses rather than beats.

Sing this song by Canadian composer John Beckwith as a practical experience in the performance of a hybrid duple time composition. Practise the conducting pattern for duple time (down on beat 1, up on beat 2), while singing the song.

The Man of Thessaly

John Beckwith
(1927-   )

Copyright 1964 BMI Canada Limited. Used by permission of Berandol Music Limited.

*In hybrid time compositions, the composer may insert a dotted vertical line within each measure to facilitate reading.

EXERCISES ON HYBRID DUPLE TIME

1. For each of the following melodies:
   (i) name the key;
   (ii) add the time signature;
   (iii) sing the melody.

Ireland

a)

D. Paul

b)

D. Paul

c)

Czechoslovakia

d)

3 part Canon

Germany

e)

2. For each of the following melodies:
   (i) name the key;
  (ii) rewrite the melody, grouping the notes correctly according to the given time signature;
 (iii) add the necessary bar lines.

Hybrid Triple Time

In hybrid triple time there are three beats per bar, the first being stronger than the second or third. The first beat is usually a dotted note, consisting of three pulses, and the second and third beats are simple notes, each consisting of two pulses. The upper numeral of the time signature is always 7 (indicating seven pulses per bar), and the lower numeral is 2, 4, 8, or 16 (indicating the type of note that represents one pulse).

Chart of Hybrid Triple Time Signatures

Points to Remember:

1) Although there are seven pulses per bar, these pulses form *three beats.*
2) Notes of eighth value or less (♪ ♪ ♪ ♪) are beamed together if they belong to the same beat.
3) Since there is no single note equal to seven pulses, a note sustained for an entire measure must be written as three notes joined by two ties.
4) Of the four time signatures shown above, ⁷⁄₄ and ⁷⁄₈ are the most frequently used.

In hybrid triple time, the beat that includes three pulses is occasionally the second or third beat rather than the first. In either case, the notes are grouped accordingly:

Hybrid Triple Time Piano Piece

Listen to a performance of this hybrid triple time piece by the Greek composer Yannis Constantinidis. Notice that each seven-pulse measure divides into three beats (♩. ♩ ♩).

Greek Miniature, No. 13

Yannis Constantinidis
(1903-   )

Hybrid Quadruple Time

Hybrid quadruple meters are not as frequently encountered as hybrid duple or hybrid triple meters. Nonetheless, they have been used occasionally by twentieth century composers. By definition, a hybrid quadruple meter is one that has four beats per bar and includes both simple beats and compound beats. Study the following examples of rhythmic patterns in hybrid quadruple time.

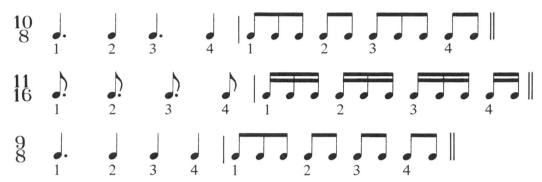

Hybrid Quadruple Time Melody

Play the following melody as a practical experience in the performance of music in hybrid quadruple time.

EXERCISES ON HYBRID TIME SIGNATURES

1. For each of the following melodies:
   (i) name the key;
   (ii) add the time signature;
   (iii) clap the rhythm while counting the beats aloud;
   (iv) sing the melody.

102

2. For each of the following melodies:
   (i) name the key;
   (ii) rewrite the melody, grouping the notes correctly according to the given time signature;
   (iii) add the necessary bar lines.

M. de Falla

a)

Croatia

b)

Fine

D.C. al Fine

RESTS IN HYBRID METERS

A Rest For an Entire Bar

A whole rest is used to indicate an entire measure of silence in *any* meter.

Examples: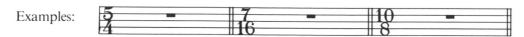

Rests of Two Beats

In hybrid duple time, the whole rest represents two beats of silence. In hybrid *triple* time, each beat of a two-beat silence is written separately.

In hybrid *quadruple* time, a silence of two beats must be represented by a single rest when the silence begins on the first or third beat of the bar and when the two beats of silence are either both simple or both compound.

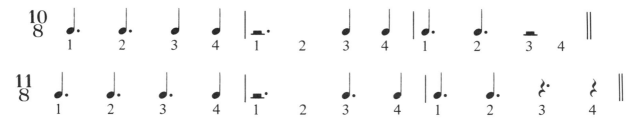

Rests of One Beat

In all hybrid meters, a single rest is used to express one beat of silence.

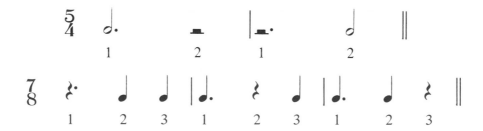

In older editions of music, one compound beat of silence is sometimes expressed by two rests, but this practice is now considered "old fashioned" and *you are advised to avoid it.*

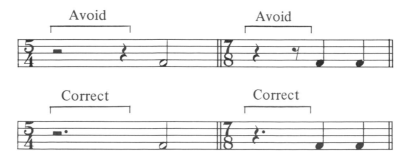

Rests of Less Than One Beat

The rules for completing the time of individual *simple* beats in hybrid meters are the same as those outlined in the Simple Time chapter of *Sound & Symbol*, Volume I (page 156). Beats are completed in such a way that the division of the simple beat into two pulses can be clearly seen.

simple
beat

The rules for completing the time of individual *compound* beats in hybrid meters are the same as those outlined in the Compound Time chapter of *Sound & Symbol*, Volume I (page 194). Beats are completed in such a way that the division of the compound beat into three pulses can be clearly seen.

compound
beat

EXERCISES ON RESTS IN HYBRID METERS

1. Add rests beneath the brackets to complete each of the following measures.

106

Further Exercises

1. For each of the following thematic excerpts in hybrid time:
   (i) add the time signature;
   (ii) play the excerpt.

Symphony No. 3, 2nd mvt.

Piano Sonata No. 1, 3rd mvt.

Piano Sonata No. 7, 3rd mvt.

Neptune the Mystic from The Planets

Russian Easter Festival Overture

Pantomime from El Amor Brujo

IRREGULAR NOTE GROUPS

P I II |*The Triplet*|

A triplet is an irregular group consisting of *three* notes that are played or sung in the time of *two* notes of the same type. Triplets are found most frequently in meters whose beats divide into two pulses (i.e., in simple time).

A triplet is written as three notes of the same value. A small 3 close to the noteheads (with or without a slur or bracket) or at the beam (usually without a slur or bracket) indicates that three notes of equal value are to be played in the time of two.

Examples:

A triplet is not always equal to one beat. In the following thematic excerpt in ⅔ time, three sixteenth notes are played in the time of two. This triplet is therefore equal to *half* a beat.

F. Mendelssohn

A triplet figure occasionally contains two notes rather than three. It is still counted and felt as three pulses, but, as in the following example, the first note of the triplet represents two pulses, while the second note represents one pulse.

E. Grieg

Triplets occasionally include a dotted rhythm. In the following example, the first note of each triplet represents one and a half pulses, the second note, half a pulse, and the third note, one pulse. Play this example on the piano.

Portugal

Piano Piece with Triplets

Listen to a performance of this harpsichord sonata by Domenico Scarlatti. Notice the almost continuous triplet rhythm that divides each beat into three pulses rather than two. (The symbols indicating the triplet rhythm — slurs, brackets, and 3's — are omitted in some editions of music once the triplet rhythm has been established.)

Harpsichord Sonata, Longo 83

Domenico Scarlatti
(1685-1757)

Melody with Triplets

Play (or sing and play) the following melody as a practical experience in the performance of triplets.

Ständchen

Franz Schubert
(1797-1828)

P I II EXERCISES ON TRIPLETS

1. For each of the following melodies:
   (i) name the key;
   (ii) add the time signature;
   (iii) clap the rhythm;
   (iv) sing the melody.

France

Germany

England

K. Goldmark

Flanders

e)

2. Add bar lines, then play each of the following melodies.

G. Verdi

a)

S. Yradier

3. For each of the following thematic excerpts:
  (i) add the time signature;
  (ii) play the excerpt.

Overture to Tannhäuser

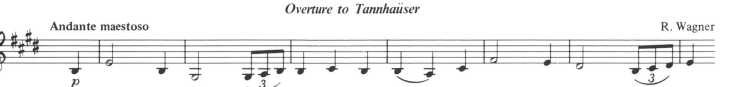

Piano Trio No. 3, 1st mvt.

Cello Concerto No. 9, 1st mvt.

Symphony No. 9 ("The Great"), 4th mvt.

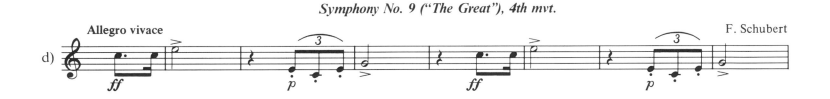

Symphony No. 45 ("Farewell"), 5th mvt.

Cello Concerto No. 1, 1st mvt.

String Quintet No. 11, 1st mvt.

OTHER IRREGULAR NOTE GROUPS

The Duplet

A *duplet* is an irregular group consisting of *two* notes that are played or sung in the time of *three* notes of the same type. Duplets are used in meters whose beats divide into three pulses (i.e., in compound time).

A duplet is written as two notes of the same value. A small 2 close to the noteheads (with or without a slur or bracket) or at the beam (usually without a slur or bracket) indicates that the two notes are to be played in the time of three.

Study the following excerpt from a piano composition in compound triple time. Notice the duplets in measures 3 and 8. Each of these duplets consists of two eighth notes played in the time of three. Each duplet represents one beat.

Claire de lune

C. Debussy

(etc.)

The Quadruplet

A quadruplet is an irregular group consisting of *four* notes. Quadruplets are often found in compound meters, where the beat normally divides into three pulses. If a composer wishes to compress *four* pulses into the time of *three*, he will write a *quadruplet*. A quadruplet contains four notes of equal value written with a small 4 close to the noteheads, or at the beam.

Study the following folk song in compound duple time. Here the quadruplets consist of four eighth notes performed in the time of three. Each quadruplet equals one beat.

A composer will occasionally write a quadruplet consisting of four notes that are played in the time of six. This is the case in bars 2, 4, and 6 of the following thematic excerpt.

The Quintuplet, Sextuplet, and Septuplet

Each of these irregular groups can be played in the time of four notes. In compound time, the quintuplet and septuplet are occasionally played in the time of six notes, while in simple time, the septuplet is occasionally played in the time of eight notes. Study the following examples.

Quintuplets: 5 sixteenth notes in the time of 4:

Sextuplets: 6 sixteenth notes in the time of 4:

L. Boccherini

Septuplets: 7 thirty-second notes in the time of 4:

I. Stravinsky

Irregular groups of nine, ten, eleven and twelve notes are also possible. When solving irregular groups, remember:

1) The number marked within the slur or across the beam of the irregular group indicates the number of notes in that group.
2) You may deduce the time in which the irregular note group is to be played by considering both the time signature and the total value of the other beats in the bar.

II | EXERCISES ON IRREGULAR GROUPS |

1. For each of the following melodies:
   (i) name the key;
   (ii) write the time signature(s);
   (iii) clap the rhythm;
   (iv) sing the melody.

America

a)

Mexico

b)

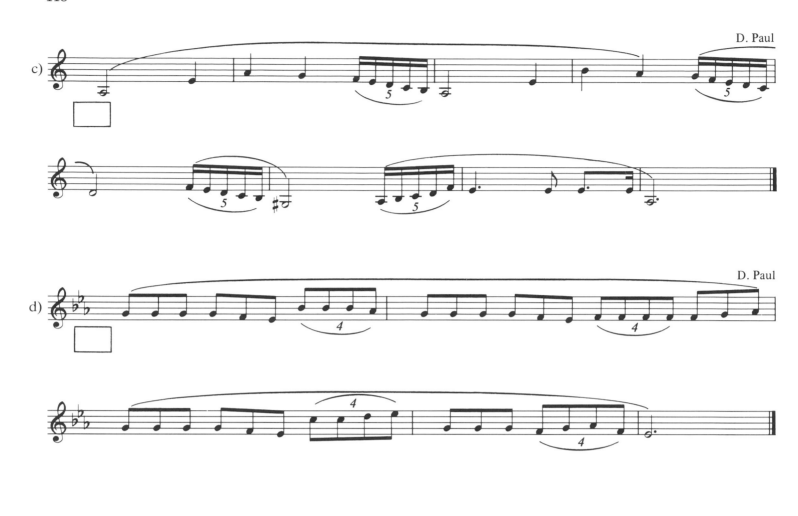

c) D. Paul

d) D. Paul

2. For each of the following thematic excerpts:
   (i) add the time signature;
   (ii) play the excerpt.

Meditation from Thaïs

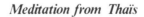

a) J. Massenet

Arabian Dance from The Nutcracker Suite

P.I. Tchaikovsky

b)

Symphony No. 6, 2nd mvt.

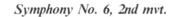

P.I. Tchaikovsky

c)

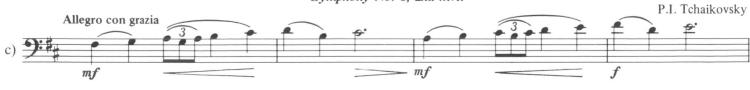

Prélude from Suite algérienne

C. Saint-Saëns

Karelia Suite, 3rd mvt.

J. Sibelius

Chinese Dance from The Nutcracker Suite

P.I. Tchaikovsky

Lyric Piece, Op. 43, No. 6

E. Grieg

Symphony No. 5, 2nd mvt.

P.I. Tchaikovsky

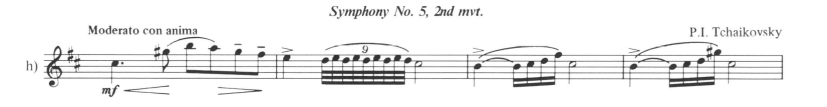

Danse grèque from Les Erinnyes

J. Massenet

5. FURTHER MEANS OF PITCH ORGANIZATION

Für Elise

Ludwig van Beethoven
(1770-1827)

In this excerpt from Beethoven's "Für Elise", a piano piece in A−, the raised leading note, G♯, appears frequently. The note D♯ also occurs several times. Although D♯ is not a note in the scale of A−, these D♯'s do not oppose the key since they are used to lead into and emphasize E, the dominant of A−.

A note that does not belong to the key in which a passage is written is called a *chromatic note*. A complete series of chromatic notes is found in a *chromatic scale*.

CHROMATIC NOTES AND CHROMATIC SCALES

Chromatic Notes in Major Keys

In any major key, notes forming the scale are called *diatonic*. Composers do not necessarily limit themselves to these diatonic notes when writing in a particular key. They often add decorating notes that do not belong to the key. These *chromatic* notes are easily identified in the major mode because each of them requires an accidental.

Chromatic notes that pull upward are usually spelled as *raised* scale notes. A numeral "slashed" with an arrow pointing upward indicates the scale degree that has been raised (e.g., ∕⁷ in D+ indicates D♯). Play the following melody.

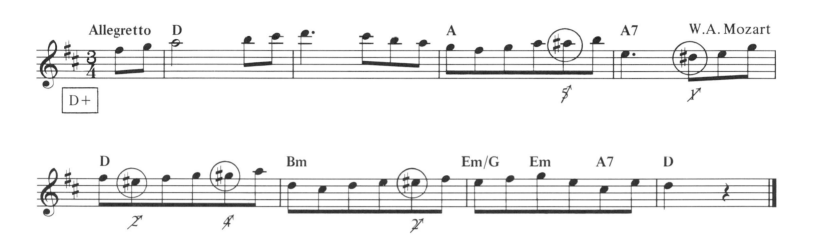

Chromatic notes that pull downward are usually spelled as *lowered* scale notes. A numeral "slashed" with an arrow pointing downward indicates the scale degree that has been lowered (e.g., ⑥ in D♭+ indicates B♭♭). Play the following melody.

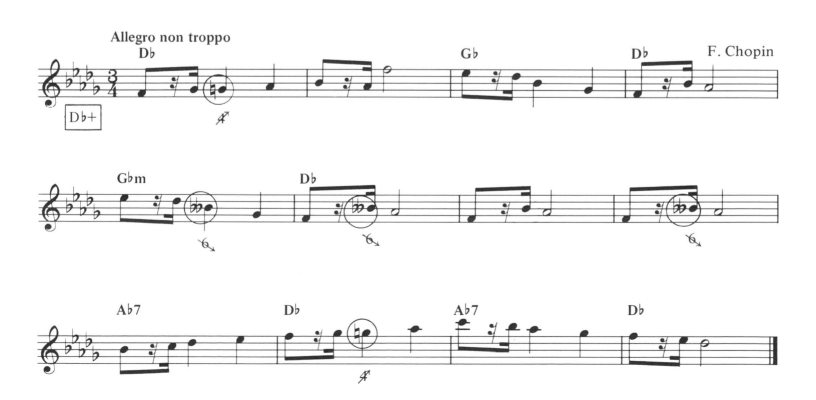

Chromatic Note Song in the Major Mode

The following song in Ab+ contains chromatic notes A (X̷), B (2̷), and F♯ (6̷). Sing the melody as a practical experience in the performance of a major mode composition containing chromatic notes.

Waltz from La Traviata

Giuseppe Verdi
(1813-1901)

Chromatic Scales in the Major Mode

A chromatic scale is one that proceeds exclusively by semitone. A chromatic scale is actually a diatonic scale with chromatic notes added. The resulting scale contains every semitone within the octave.

When asked to write a chromatic scale in the *major* mode, you should:

1) Write the major scale.

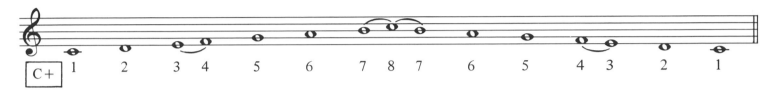

2) Fill in the semitones between scale steps 1 and 2, 2 and 3, 4 and 5, 5 and 6, and 6 and 7. In the ascending form of the scale, this is done by inserting the raised tonic, supertonic, subdominant, dominant, and submediant immediately following the appearance of each in its diatonic form. Similarly, in the descending form of the scale, the lowered leading note, submediant, dominant, mediant, and supertonic are inserted immediately following the appearance of each in its diatonic form. Thus, five chromatic notes are used in the ascending form and five in the descending form of the chromatic scale.*

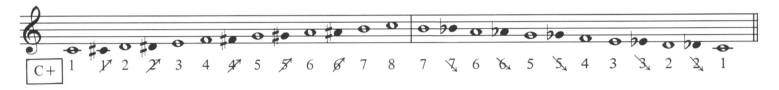

In keys with three or more *sharps,* an *ascending* chromatic scale will contain one or more notes with *double sharps.*

Example:

In keys with three or more *flats,* a *descending* chromatic scale will contain one or more notes with *double flats.*

Example:

* The chromatic scale shown above is used to create both *melody* and *harmony* in the major mode. Some approaches to teaching chromatic scales differentiate between the spelling of a *melodic chromatic* and a *harmonic chromatic* scale. Many theorists and teachers, however, do not make this distinction, but rather use a single chromatic scale as described above.

II | EXERCISES ON CHROMATIC SCALES IN THE MAJOR MODE |

1. Produce the specified chromatic scales by adding a clef, a key signature, and any necessary accidentals to each of the following series of notes.

a)

| D + |

b)

| Bb+ |

c)

| G+ |

d)
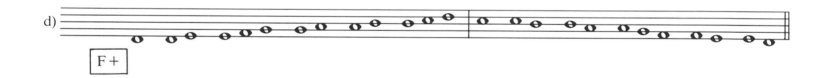

| F + |

e)

| A+ |

f)
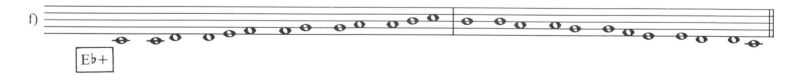

| Eb+ |

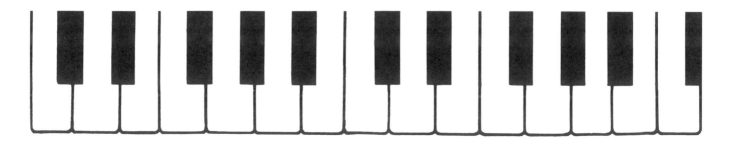

2. For each of the following major keys:
- (i) add the key signature;
- (ii) write the *major* scale ascending and descending;
- (iii) add the chromatic notes necessary to produce a chromatic scale.

a) 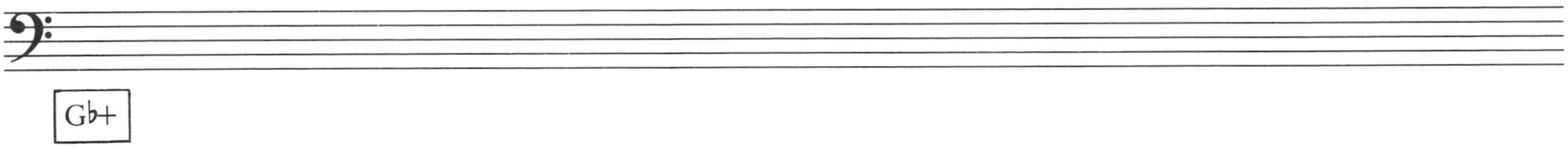 $\mathbf{\mathcal{9}\colon}$

Gb+

b) 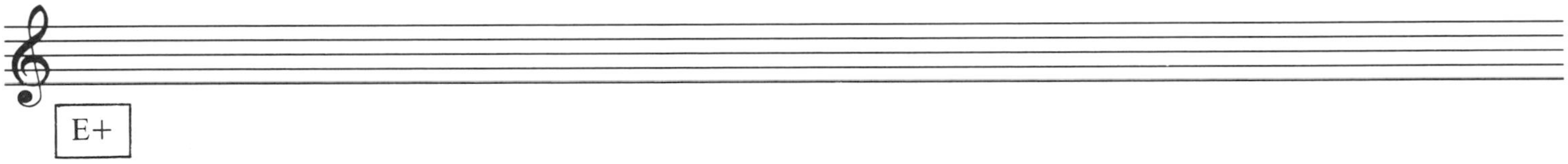 $\&$

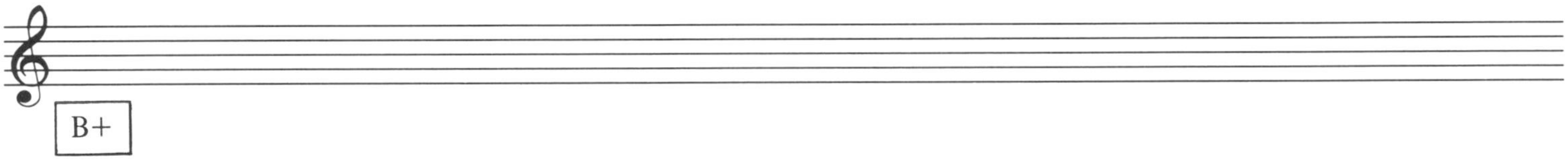

E+

c) 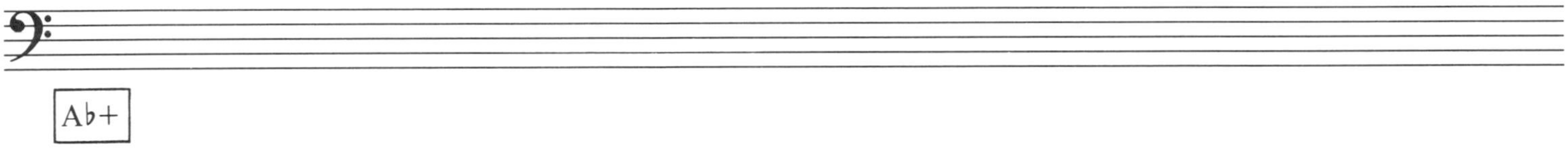 $\mathbf{\mathcal{9}\colon}$

Ab+

d) $\&$

B+

e) $\mathbf{\mathcal{9}\colon}$

Db+

f) 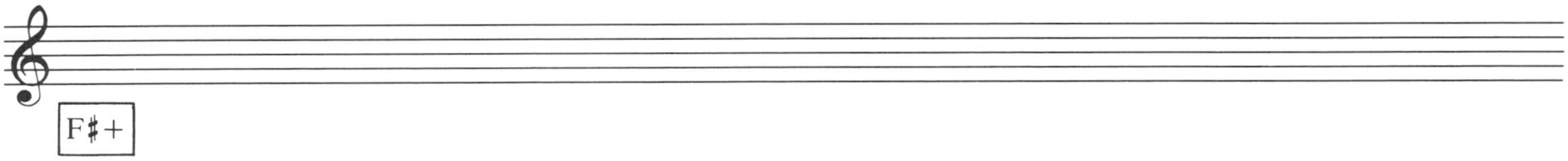 $\&$

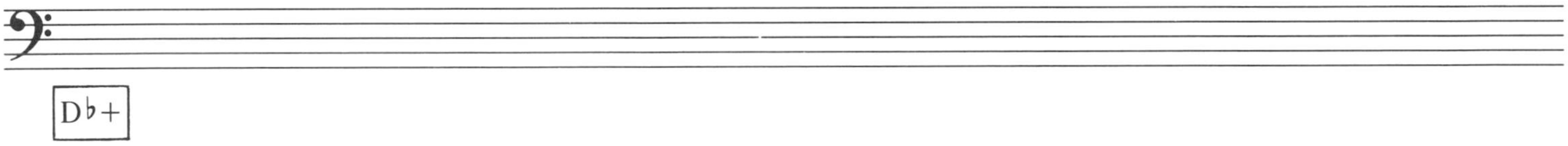

F#+

II EXERCISES ON MELODIC UNITS AND TWO-PART TEXTURES

1. For each of the following thematic excerpts:
  (i) name the key;
  (ii) circle each chromatic note;
  (iii) write a "slashed" numeral beneath each chromatic note to indicate the scale degree that has been raised or lowered;
  (iv) play the excerpt.

Divertimento, K. 247, 3rd mvt.

W.A. Mozart

Violin Concerto No. 1, 3rd mvt.

N. Paganini

Clarinet Concerto, 3rd mvt.

W.A. Mozart

Golliwog's Cakewalk from The Children's Corner

C. Debussy

At the Hearth, Op. 15, No. 8

R. Schumann

Symphony No. 1, 3rd mvt.

F. Schubert

Transcendental Etude No. 7 ("Eroica")

F. Liszt

Symphonic Poem No. 3 ("Les Préludes")

F. Liszt

Symphony No. 92 ("Oxford"), 4th mvt.

F.J. Haydn

Hungarian Rhapsody No. 13

F. Liszt

Piano Sonata No. 10, 1st mvt.

L. van Beethoven

Grand galop chromatique

F. Liszt

Song of India from Sadko

N. Rimsky-Korsakov

2. For each of the following melodies:
  (i) name the key;
  (ii) circle each chromatic note;
  (iii) write a "slashed" numeral beneath each chromatic note to indicate the scale degree that has been raised or lowered;
  (iv) sing the melody.

3. For each of the following duets:

  (i) name the key;

 (ii) sing each part;

(iii) play the duet on the piano;

(iv) circle each chromatic note;

 (v) name each harmonic interval that includes a chromatic note;

(vi) sing the duet with a friend.

Chromatic Notes in Minor Keys

In any minor key, notes forming the natural, harmonic, or melodic minor scale are called *diatonic*. Even notes that have accidentals are considered diatonic as long as they are found in one of these three scale forms. Thus, the raised 7th degree in the harmonic minor and the raised or lowered 6th and 7th degrees in the melodic minor are diatonic notes.

In a given key, notes that are *not* diatonic are called *chromatic*. Since all chromatic notes include accidentals, it is important to recognize which notes with accidentals are diatonic and which are chromatic.

Notes that pull upward are usually spelled as *raised* scale notes. Play the following melody.

Notes that pull downward are usually spelled as *lowered* scale notes. Play the following melody.

Chromatic Note Song in the Minor Mode

The following song in E— contains the chromatic notes F (♮) and A♯ (♯). Sing the melody as a practical experience in the performance of a minor mode composition containing chromatic notes.

Der Müller und der Bach

Franz Schubert
(1797-1828)

Mässig (Moderately)

E— Wo ein treu-es Her-ze in Lie - be ver-geht, da wel-ken die
Where true love re-ject-ed sinks in deep___ de - spair, Then nev - er a -

Li -lien auf je - dem___ Beet. Da muss in die Wol - ken der
gain will the li - lies bloom there. And then in a cloud-bank the

Voll - mond geh'n da-mit sei - ne Thrä - nen die Men - schen nicht
moon ___ dis-ap-pears That men may per - ceive not a trace_ of___ her___

seh'n, _____ da hal - ten die Eng - lein die Au - gen sich
tears. _____ The an - gels their eyes_____ in sor - row will

zu, und schluch -zen und sin - gen die See - le zur Ruh.
close, And lull with a re - qui - em the soul_____ to re - pose.

Chromatic Scales in the Minor Mode

In the minor mode, a chromatic scale is written by adding chromatic notes to the *complete* series of diatonic notes belonging to the given key (i.e., notes from the natural, harmonic, and melodic minor scales).

When asked to write a chromatic scale in the *minor* mode, you should:
1) Write the complete series of diatonic notes in the minor scale.

2) Fill in the semitones between scale steps 1 and 2, 3 and 4, and 4 and 5. In the ascending form of the scale, this is done by inserting the raised tonic, mediant, and subdominant immediately following the appearance of each in its diatonic form. In the descending form of the scale, the lowered dominant, subdominant, and supertonic are inserted immediately following the appearance of each in its diatonic form. Thus, three chromatic notes are used in the ascending form and three in the descending form of the chromatic scale.*

In keys with three or more *sharps,* an *ascending* chromatic scale will contain one or more notes with *double sharps.*
Example:

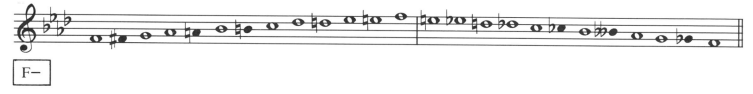

In keys with four or more *flats,* a *descending* chromatic scale will contain one or more notes with *double flats.*
Example:

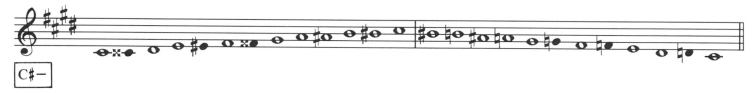

You have seen that there is a raised form for the ascending portion and a lowered form for the descending portion of a chromatic scale. In composed music, notes taken from the raised form are occasionally used in descending passages, and, less frequently, notes taken from the lowered form are used in ascending passages. In either case, the composer may have wanted to simplify the appearance of the music or avoid accidentals that are distant from the key. For example:

N. Rimsky-Korsakov

*The chromatic scale shown above is used to create both *melody* and *harmony* in the minor mode. Some approaches to teaching chromatic scales differentiate between the spelling of a *melodic chromatic* and a *harmonic chromatic* scale. Many theorists and teachers, however, do not make this distinction, but rather use a single chromatic scale as described above.

EXERCISES ON CHROMATIC SCALES IN THE MINOR MODE

1. Produce the specified chromatic scales by adding a clef, a minor mode key signature, and any necessary accidentals to the following series of notes.

a)

C−

b)

B−

c)

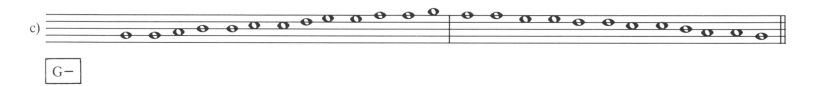

G−

d)

E−

e)

D−

f)

F♯−

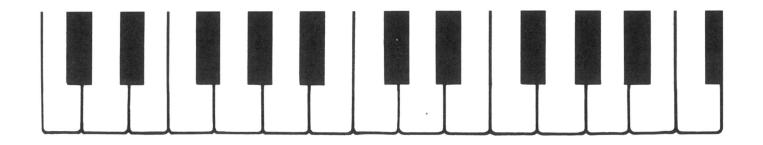

2. For each of the following minor keys:
   (i) add the key signature;
  (ii) write the complete series of diatonic notes, ascending and descending, found in the scale;
 (iii) add the chromatic notes necessary to produce a chromatic scale.

a) 𝄢

C♯−

b) 𝄢

B♭−

c) 𝄞

G♯−

d) 𝄞

F−

e) 𝄞

D♯−

f) 𝄢

E♭−

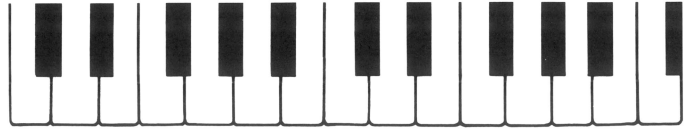

EXERCISES ON MELODIC UNITS AND ON TWO- AND FOUR-PART TEXTURES

1. For each of the following thematic excerpts:
  (i) name the key;
  (ii) circle each chromatic note;
  (iii) write a "slashed" numeral beneath each chromatic note to indicate the scale degree that has been raised or lowered;
  (iv) play the excerpt.

Rondo Capriccioso

F. Mendelssohn

Violin Concerto No. 8, 1st mvt.

L. Spohr

Piano Sonata No. 19, 1st mvt.

L. van Beethoven

Horn Trio, Op. 40, 3rd mvt.

J. Brahms

Harpsichord Concerto No. 5, 1st mvt.

J.S. Bach

Violin Caprice, Op. 1, No. 15

N. Paganini

Piano Concerto No. 1, 3rd mvt.

E. MacDowell

g)

marcatissimo ma leggiero

Etude, Op. 10, No. 2

F. Chopin

h)

2. For each of the following melodies:
   (i) name the key;
   (ii) circle each chromatic note;
   (iii) write a "slashed" numeral beneath each chromatic note to indicate the scale degree that has been raised or lowered;
   (iv) sing the melody.

America

a)

Greece

b)

F. Chopin

c)

3. For each of the following duets:
   (i) name the key;
  (ii) sing each part;
 (iii) play the duet on the piano;
 (iv) circle each interval that includes a chromatic note;
  (v) name each harmonic interval containing an accidental;
 (vi) sing the duet with a friend.

4. For the following chorale setting:
   (i) circle each chromatic note;
  (ii) sing each of the four parts in the octave that is most comfortable for your voice;
 (iii) prepare a performance in four-part vocal harmony with three fellow students.

MODAL SCALES AND MODAL MELODIES

The Church Modes

The church, or ecclesiastical, modes are a system of scales used by composers of the Middle Ages and Renaissance as series of notes from which to draw in creating their compositions. Each church mode consists of the notes of the C+ scale, but each has a different starting note. Each church mode therefore has a specific arrangement of tones and semitones. In the twentieth century, some composers have returned to the church modes as a basis of pitch organization.

Interval Structures and Names of the Church Modes

The interval structures of the various church modes may be learned by referring to the white notes on the piano. The order of tones and semitones produced by playing the white notes from C to C results in the *Ionian mode.* The Ionian mode is identical in structure to the major scale:

C   D   E ‿ F   G   A   B ‿ C.

D to D, using only white notes, produces the *Dorian mode.* The Dorian mode is identical in structure to the natural minor scale with raised 6th degree:

D   E ‿ F   G   A   B ‿ C   D.

E to E produces the *Phrygian mode.* The Phrygian mode is identical in structure to the natural minor scale with flattened 2nd degree:

E ‿ F   G   A   B ‿ C   D   E.

F to F produces the *Lydian mode.* The Lydian mode is identical in structure to the major scale with raised 4th degree:

F   G   A   B ‿ C   D   E ‿ F.

G to G produces the *Mixolydian mode.* The Mixolydian mode is identical in structure to the major scale with flattened 7th degree:

G   A   B ‿ C   D   E ‿ F   G.

A to A produces the *Aeolian mode.* The Aeolian mode is identical in structure to the natural minor scale:

A   B ‿ C   D   E ‿ F   G   A.

B to B produces the rarely-used *Locrian mode:*

B ‿ C   D   E ‿ F   G   A   B.

In the church modes, the starting (and ending) note of the scale is called the *finalis* rather than the tonic. Each of these church modes is categorized by the name of its finalis followed by the name of the mode. The scale from D to D (using only the white notes on the piano) is called *D Dorian.* E to E is called *E Phrygian,* F to F is called *F Mixolydian,* and so on.

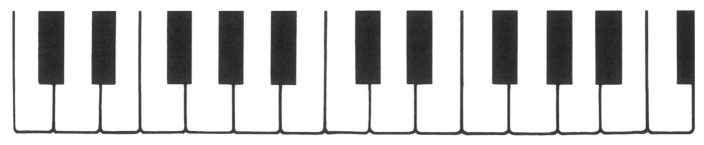

Church Modes Similar in Structure to the Major Mode

Ionian Mode

Since the Ionian mode is identical in structure to the major mode, an Ionian scale has the same key signature as a major scale with the same starting note (i.e., the parallel major). Whether a melody is referred to as *major* or *Ionian* normally depends on the historical period in which it was written. If the melody was composed during the Middle Ages or Renaissance it is usually referred to as Ionian. A similar melody written in a later historical period is referred to as major.

Examples of Ionian scales:

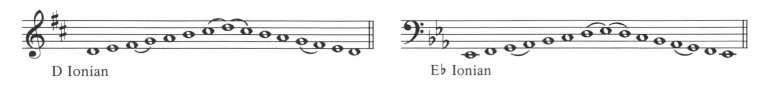

D Ionian   Eb Ionian

Sing the following song as an introduction to the sound of music written in the Ionian mode. It was composed by Adam de la Halle in the late thirteenth century for the medieval play, *Robin et Marion.*

Adam de la Halle

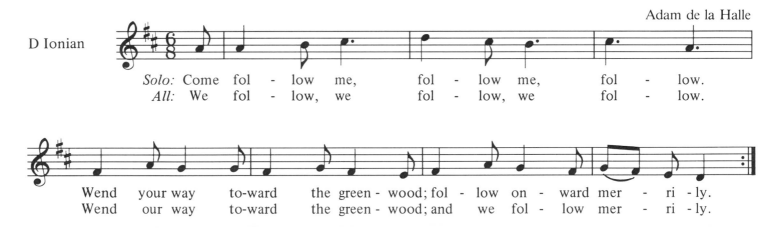

D Ionian

Solo: Come fol - low me, fol - low me, fol - low.
All: We fol - low, we fol - low, we fol - low.

Wend your way to-ward the green - wood; fol - low on - ward mer - ri - ly.
Wend our way to-ward the green - wood; and we fol - low mer - ri - ly.

Lydian Mode

A Lydian scale sounds like a major scale with its 4th degree raised one semitone. In sharp keys, a Lydian scale is usually written with the same key signature as its parallel major. An accidental is used to raise the 4th degree one semitone. In flat keys, a key signature of *one flat less* than that of the parallel major is used.

Examples of Lydian scales:

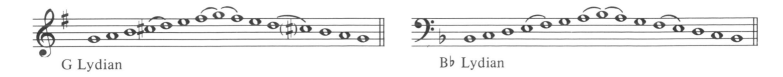

G Lydian   Bb Lydian

Sing the following medieval part-song as an introduction to the sound of music written in the Lydian mode.

England

F Lydian

Might - y Lord, gra - cious Lord, ev - er be Thy name a - dored!

Lov - ing Lord, help - ful Lord, grant us, by Thy grace re - stored, __

Hea - ven's joy as our re - ward __ af - ter earth - ly days.

Hear us sing in __ sweet ac - cord __ songs of love and praise.

Mixolydian Mode

A Mixolydian scale sounds like a major scale with its 7th degree lowered one semitone. In flat keys, a Mixolydian scale is usually written with the same key signature as its parallel major. An accidental is used to lower the 7th degree one semitone. In sharp keys, a key signature of *one sharp less* than that of the parallel major is used.

Examples of Mixolydian scales:

Bb Mixolydian

D Mixolydian

Sing the following example of Gregorian Chant as an introduction to the sound of music written in the Mixolydian mode.

Gregorian Chant

G Mixolydian

Church Modes Similar in Structure to the Minor Mode

Aeolian Mode

Since the Aeolian mode is identical in structure to the natural minor mode, an Aeolian scale is written with the same key signature as its parallel natural minor. Whether a melody is referred to as *natural minor* or *Aeolian* normally depends on the historical period in which it was written. If the melody was composed during the Middle Ages or Renaissance, it is usually referred to as Aeolian. A similar melody written in a later historical period is referred to as minor.

Examples of Aeolian scales:

C♯ Aeolian   G Aeolian

Sing the following folk song as an introduction to the sound of music written in the Aeolian mode.

Dorian Mode

A Dorian scale sounds like a natural minor scale with its 6th degree raised one semitone. In sharp keys, a Dorian scale is written with the same key signature as its parallel natural minor. An accidental is used to raise the 6th degree one semitone. In flat keys, a key signature of *one flat less* than that of the parallel natural minor is used.

Examples of Dorian scales:

B Dorian   C Dorian

Sing the following folk song as an introduction to the sound of music written in the Dorian mode.

Phrygian Mode

A Phrygian scale sounds like a natural minor scale with its 2nd degree lowered one semitone. In flat keys, a Phrygian scale is written with the same key signature as its parallel natural minor. An accidental is used to lower the 2nd degree one semitone. In sharp keys, a key signature of *one sharp less* than that of the parallel natural minor is used.

Examples of Phrygian scales:

Sing the following melody as an introduction to the sound of music written in the Phrygian mode.

144

EXERCISES ON MODAL SCALES

1. Write the following modal scales, both ascending and descending, using the clef of your choice and the correct key signature for each. Add any necessary accidentals.

a)

| E Dorian

b)

| B♭ Mixolydian

c)

| A Phrygian

d)

| F Dorian

e)

| B Aeolian

f)

| A♭ Ionian

g)

| E Lydian

h)

| D Phrygian

i)

| E♭ Mixolydian

j)

| C♯ Aeolian

EXERCISES ON MELODIC UNITS

1. For each of the following modal melodies:
   (i) name the finalis and the mode;
   (ii) sing the melody.

2. For each of the following modal melodies:
    (i) add a clef, a key signature, and any accidentals necessary to produce the specified mode;
    (ii) play the melody.

o

PENTATONIC AND WHOLE-TONE SCALES, ATONALITY, AND TWELVE-TONE TECHNIQUE

Pentatonic Scales

A scale consisting of five notes is called a *pentatonic* scale. There are many five-note series that form pentatonic scales, but one of the most common can be seen by playing only the black notes on the piano. A pentatonic scale using only these black notes is F♯ G♯ A♯ C♯ D♯.

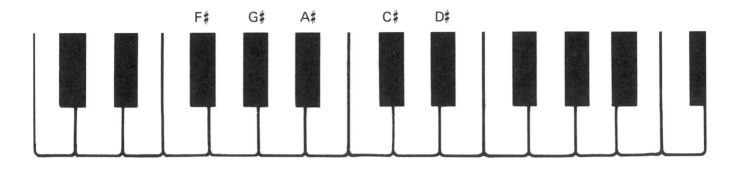

Pentatonic Song

The following traditional Appalachian song is based on a pentatonic scale with the same interval structure as that of the scale shown above, but it begins with the note G (G A B D E). Sing (or sing and play) this song as a practical experience in the performance of a pentatonic melody.

Amazing Grace

Whole-Tone Scales

A *whole-tone* scale is one that consists exclusively of whole-tone steps. When enharmonic respellings are discounted, there are essentially only two series of notes that yield the whole-tone scale.

Examples of whole-tone scales:

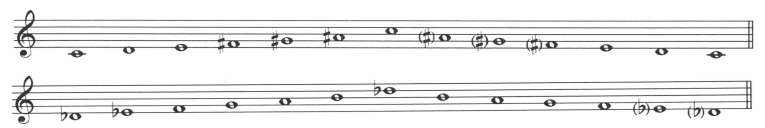

Notice that although whole-tone scales contain only whole tones, one of these whole tones must be spelled as a diminished 3rd.

Whole-Tone Song

The following song is based on the first whole-tone scale shown above, except that the A♯ is spelled as B♭. Play the melody of this song on the piano as an introduction to the sound of music based on a whole-tone scale.

In Flanders Fields

Text by John McCrae

Music by D. Paul

(over)

O Atonality and Twelve-Tone Technique

Early in the twentieth century, composers began creating music that was neither tonal (based on the major-minor scale system), nor modal (based on the church modes), nor pentatonic (based on five-note scale patterns), nor whole-tone (based on whole-tone scales). This music was designed to avoid any sense of tonality (key) and was therefore called *atonal*. In atonal music, all twelve notes within the octave are considered to be of equal importance. (Tonal music, in contrast, stresses the hierarchy of relationships among notes of the scale, the most important note being the tonic.) Composers of atonal music deliberately avoid *tertian harmony* (chords built in 3rds) and often write melodies in an angular rather than a lyrical style. The general impression created by atonal music is one of extreme dissonance and heightened expression.

Arnold Schoenberg (1874 - 1951) invented a highly structured method for composing atonally called the *twelve-tone technique*. In this technique, the twelve notes available within the octave are presented in a numbered order, and this order is maintained throughout the composition. The twelve-note pattern itself is called a *tone row*. Consecutive notes within the tone row may appear in a linear manner, as melody, or vertically, as harmony. They may also occur in *retrograde* (when the order of the original row is reversed), in *inversion* (when the direction of each interval of the original row is reversed), or in *retrograde inversion* (when the order of the inverted form is reversed).

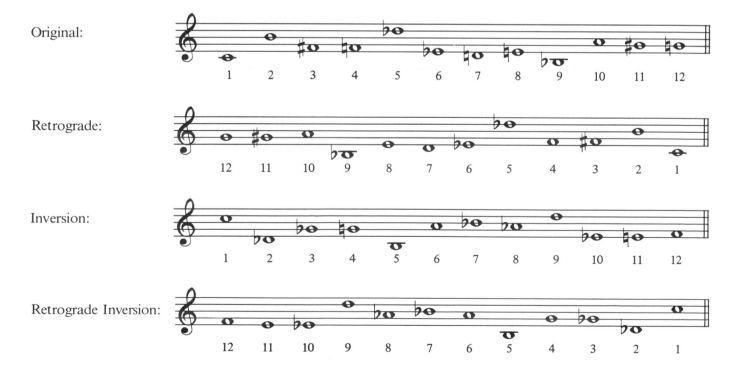

In addition, the four forms of the row may be shifted upward or downward to begin on *any* note, as long as the interval structure of the original row is preserved.

Twelve-Tone Piano Piece

Listen to a performance of the following short piano piece in order to experience the sound of a composition based on a twelve-tone row. (Only the original form of the row shown above is used.) This piece illustrates another principle of twelve-tone composition, i.e., that notes of the tone row may appear in any register.

Interlude

David Paul

O | EXERCISES ON MELODIC UNITS |

1. For each of the following thematic excerpts:
  (i) indicate whether the excerpt is modal, pentatonic, whole-tone, or twelve-tone;
  (ii) in the case of a modal theme, name the mode;
 (iii) play the excerpt.

To The Lands Over Yonder

I ___ long   to ___ go   to ___ them,   to the lands o - ver

yon - der,   to those far - thest from us,   out of sight,   out of sight,

Nuages from Nocturnes

Variations for Flute, Oboe, and Harpsichord

Polovetsian Dances from Prince Igor

Symphonie gaspésienne

153

Prélude à l'après-midi d'un faune

Très modéré

C. Debussy

Fantasia for Orchestra

H. Somers

Allegro scherzando (vivace)

The Star Shone Down

J. Coulthard

Andante semplice

In a man-ger low - ly Lay the babe so ho - ly, ho - ly, so ho - ly.

6. TRANSPOSITION, C CLEFS, AND SCORE STUDY

March from The Nutcracker Suite

Peter Ilyich Tchaikovsky
(1840 - 1893)

This excerpt from Tchaikovsky's *Nutcracker Suite* is shown in two versions — as a score for full orchestra, and as a piano reduction. In the orchestral score, the parts for clarinets ("Clarinetto I" and "Clarinetto II") and French horns ("Corni") are not notated in G+, the key of the other instrumental parts, because clarinets and French horns are *transposing instruments.* Note also that the parts for tenor trombones ("Tromb. Tenori") and violas ("Viole") use C clefs (𝄡) rather than the treble or the bass clef.

TRANSPOSITION

Transposition is the notation or performance of a piece of music in a key, clef, or octave other than that in which it was originally written. In the following example, "London Bridge" is first presented in F+. It is then transposed down a perfect 4th, into C+, and down a minor 7th, into G+ (changes of key). Next, it is transposed down an octave (change of octave). Finally, it is transposed down an octave, into the bass clef (changes of octave and clef). The distance between the key of the original melody and that of the transposed melody is called the *interval of transposition.*

F+   Lon-don Bridge is fall-ing down, fall-ing down, fall-ing down. Lon-don Bridge is fall-ing down my fair la-dy.

C+   Lon-don Bridge is fall-ing down, fall-ing down, fall-ing down. Lon-don Bridge is fall-ing down my fair la-dy.

G+   Lon-don Bridge is fall-ing down, fall-ing down, fall-ing down. Lon-don Bridge is fall-ing down my fair la-dy.

F+   Lon-don Bridge is fall-ing down, fall-ing down, fall-ing down. Lon-don Bridge is fall-ing down my fair la-dy.

F+   Lon-don Bridge is fall-ing down, fall-ing down, fall-ing down. Lon-don Bridge is fall-ing down my fair la-dy.

Notice that each of the versions of "London Bridge" shown above is in a major key. A melody never changes from major to minor, or from minor to major, when it is transposed. *If a given melody is major, the transposed melody will also be major, and if the given melody is minor, the transposed melody will also be minor.*

Songs are often transposed to accommodate the vocal range of a singer. Find the key for "London Bridge" that best suits your particular vocal range.

TRANSPOSITION IN MAJOR KEYS

Transposing from One Clef to Another

The simplest type of transposition involves only a change of clef. For example, a question may ask, "Transpose the following melody into the bass clef at the same pitch."

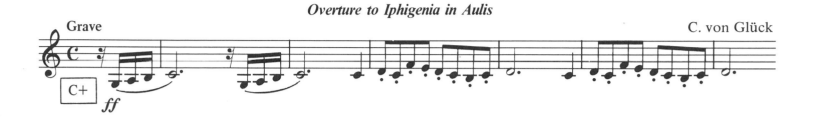

To answer this question:
1) Name the original key (C+).
2) Play the given melody.
3) Keep in mind that since this transposition involves only a change of *clef*, the transposed melody will be in the same key as the original melody and will sound exactly like it.
4) Determine the starting note of the given melody in relation to middle C. (The given melody begins on G, a 4th below middle C. The transposed melody must begin on the same G, but written in the bass clef.)
5) Rewrite the entire melody in the bass clef, keeping all the intervals and all the note names the same as in the original melody. Be sure to include performance indications such as dynamics and slurs.
6) Play the transposed melody.

Solution:

Transposing Up or Down an Octave

When you are asked to transpose music up or down an octave, remember that the *key* of the given melody will remain the same. The required interval of transposition will be a perfect 8ve. If you are asked to transpose *up* an octave, use the same key signature as in the given melody, then write each note *up* a perfect 8ve. If you are asked to transpose *down* an octave, use the same key signature as in the given melody, then write each note of the original melody *down* a perfect 8ve.

Example 1

Question: Transpose the following theme *down* an octave, using the same clef.

Eine Kleine Nachtmusik, 1st mvt.

W.A. Mozart

Solution:

W.A. Mozart

Example 2

Question: Transpose the following theme *up* an octave, using the same clef.

Piano Concerto No. 5 ("Emperor"), 1st mvt.

L. van Beethoven

Solution:

L. van Beethoven

Example 3

Question: Transpose the theme given in Example 2 *down* an octave, into the bass clef.

Solution:

L. van Beethoven

II Transposing Up, Into a New Key

Until now, you have been asked to transpose melodies without changing the keys in which they are written. In order to transpose a melody up, into a new key, you must know *either* the interval of transposition *or* the name of the new key. If the key for the transposed melody is given, the interval of transposition must be determined. On the other hand, if the interval of transposition is given, the name of the new key must be determined.

Sample question: Transpose the following melody *up* a perfect 5th.

Brandenburg Concerto No. 5, 1st mvt.

This question is asking you to transpose the melody from its original key to one a perfect 5th higher. To answer the question:

1) Name the original key (D+).

2) Play the given melody.

3) Since the interval of transposition is specified, the new key must be determined. (The required interval of transposition is a perfect 5th, and the direction of the transposition is up. Thus, the name of the new key will be a perfect 5th above the name of the original key, D+. Since the original key is major, the new key will also be major. The new key will therefore be A+.)

4) Write the name of the new key in the box below the blank staff and the interval of transposition on the line to the left of the staff. Write the proper clef, the key signature of the new key (in this case, 3 sharps), and the time signature on the staff.

5) Write each note of the given melody *up* a 5th, ensuring that all note values are exactly the same as in the original melody. *By using the correct key signature for the transposed melody, each 5th will be the required quality (in this case, perfect).*

6) Play the transposed melody.

Solution:

I Transposing Down, Into a New Key

A question may ask you to transpose a melody *down* rather than *up*. In order to transpose a melody down, into a new key, you must know *either* the name of the new key *or* the interval of transposition.

Sample Question: Transpose the following melody *down* into Bb+.

Violin Concerto No. 2, 1st mvt.

To answer this question, follow the steps outlined on page 159, keeping in mind that since the name of the new key is given, the interval of transposition must be determined. This is done by naming the interval formed between the tonic of the key of the given melody and the tonic of the key of the transposed melody.

Solution:

II | **Transposing Major Mode Melodies Containing Chromatic Notes** |

When a given melody contains chromatic notes, corresponding chromatic notes must appear in the transposed melody. Using the same procedure as that outlined in the chromatic scale section of Chapter 5 (page 121), circle each chromatic note in the given melody, then, below the staff, write a numeral "slashed" with an arrow to indicate the scale degree that has been raised or lowered. This will clarify which notes of the melody require accidentals and whether the accidentals will raise or lower notes of the scale. Transpose the melody as requested, then circle each chromatic note and add the appropriate slashed numerals.

Sample Question: Transpose the following melody *up* a major 3rd.

String Quartet, Op. 50, No. 3, 4th mvt.

Solution:

I II EXERCISES ON TRANSPOSITION IN MAJOR KEYS

1. For each of the following thematic excerpts:
   (i) name the key;
  (ii) play the excerpt;
 (iii) transpose the excerpt as instructed;
 (iv) play the transposed excerpt.

Wachet Auf

J.S. Bach

up an 8ve, using the same clef

"Toy" Symphony, 3rd mvt.

L. Mozart

down an 8ve, using the same clef

Concert royal No. 13, 4th mvt.

F. Couperin

up an 8ve, into the treble clef

Symphony No. 9 ("Choral"), 4th mvt.

L. van Beethoven

down an 8ve, using the same clef

Overture to Nabucco

Andante

G. Verdi

e)

p maestosamente

into the treble clef, at the *same pitch*

I II **2.** For each of the following thematic excerpts:
- (i) name the key;
- (ii) play the excerpt;
- (iii) name the new key and the interval of transposition;
- (iv) transpose the excerpt as instructed;
- (v) play the transposed excerpt.

Concerto Grosso, Op. 6, No. 11, 5th mvt.

Allegro

G.F. Handel

a)

up a minor 2nd

Symphony No. 1, 3rd mvt.

Presto

W.A. Mozart

b)

f

up, into G+

String Quartet, Op. 64, No. 5 ("The Lark"), 4th mvt.

Vivace

F.J. Haydn

c)

p e sempre staccato

up a minor 6th

Piano Sonata No. 23 ("Appassionata"), 1st mvt.

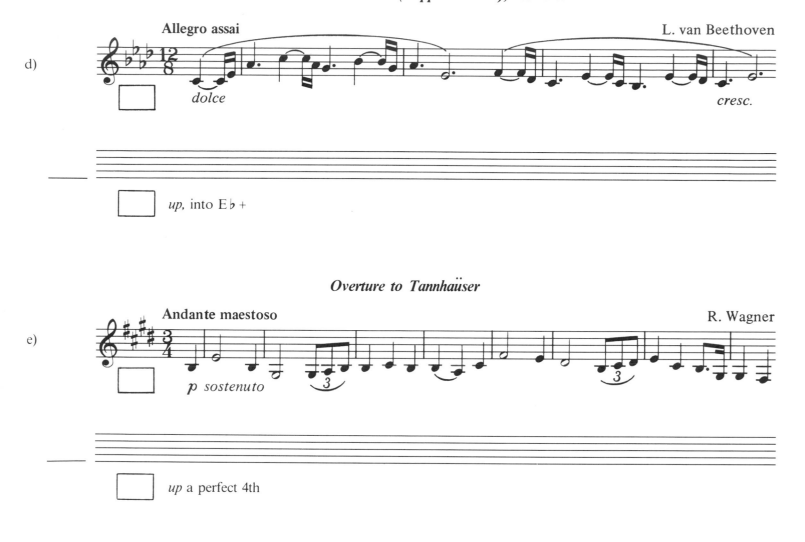

II 3. For each of the following thematic excerpts:
   (i) name the key;
   (ii) play the excerpt;
   (iii) name the new key and the interval of transposition;
   (iv) transpose the excerpt as instructed;
   (v) play the transposed excerpt.

Piano Sonata No. 5, 1st mvt.

164

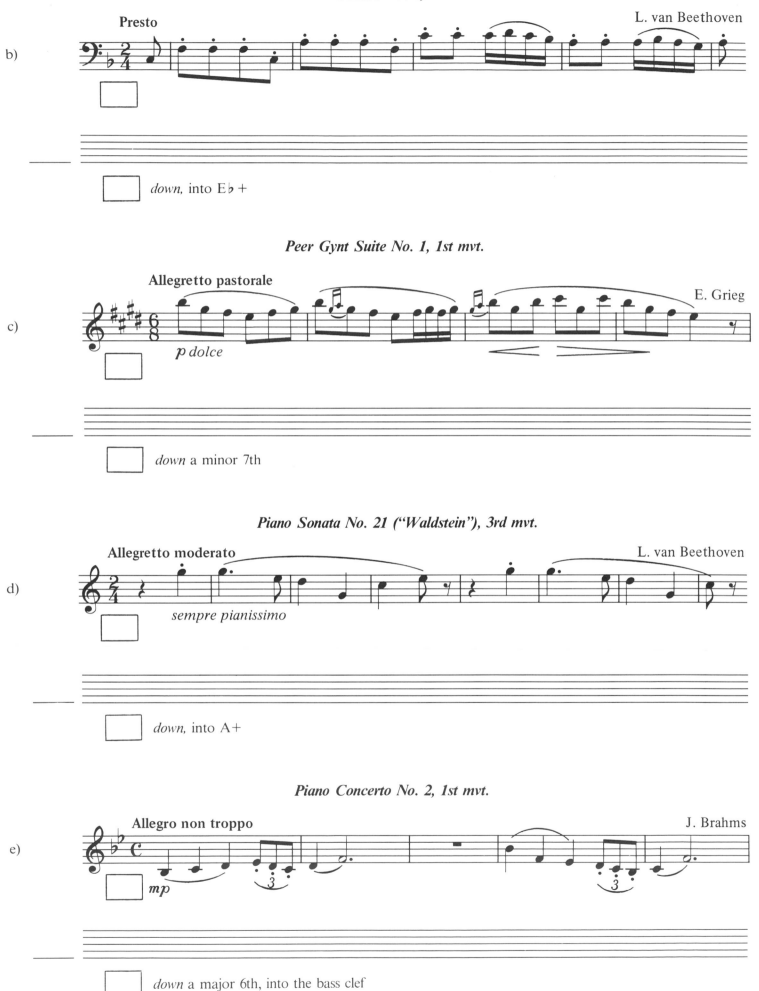

II **4.** For each of the following thematic excerpts:

   (i) name the key;

  (ii) play the excerpt;

 (iii) circle each *chromatic* note and write a "slashed" numeral beneath it to indicate the scale degree that has been raised or lowered;

 (iv) name the new key and the interval of transposition;

  (v) transpose the excerpt as instructed, indicating each chromatic note;

 (vi) play the transposed excerpt.

Piano Sonata No. 19, 2nd mvt.

W.A. Mozart

a)

up, into B♭+

Funeral Triumph of Tasso

F. Liszt

b)

down a diminished 7th

Violin Concerto, 3rd mvt.

F. Mendelssohn

c)

down, into B+

German Dance, K. 600, No. 1

W.A. Mozart

d)

up a minor 3rd

TRANSPOSITION IN MINOR KEYS

Transposing Minor Mode Melodies Without Accidentals

Transposition up or down in minor keys follows the same procedure as in major keys. To transpose a melody, you must know the name of the original key, the interval of transposition, the direction of transposition (*up* or *down*), and the name of the new key. After writing the correct key signature for the new key, transpose each note of the given melody up or down the number of steps indicated by the interval of transposition. *Remember that if a given melody is in a minor key, the transposed melody will also be minor.*

Sample Question: Transpose the following theme *down* a major 6th.

The Moldau

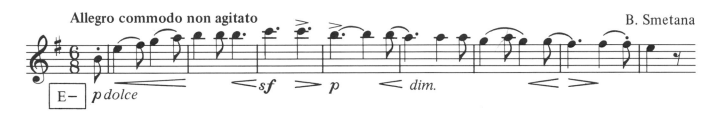

Solution:

Transposing Minor Mode Melodies Containing Diatonic Alterations

Diatonic alterations are found in the raised leading note of the harmonic minor scale and the raised and lowered 6th and 7th degrees of the melodic minor scale. If an accidental is used to alter one of these notes in a given melody, the note must be altered correspondingly in the transposed melody.

In the following sample question, the given melody in D– contains raised 7th degrees (C♯'s) from the harmonic minor scale and raised 6th and 7th degrees (B♮ and C♯) from the ascending melodic minor scale.

Sample Question: Transpose the following theme *up* a major 3rd.

Concerto for Two Violins, 3rd mvt.

To answer this question:
1) Name the original key (D-).
2) Play the melody.
3) Since the interval of transposition is specified, the new key must be determined. (Since the original key is D-, the new key will be F♯-, a major 3rd above the original key.)
4) Transpose each note *up* a 3rd from the given melody, using the key signature of F♯-, (3 sharps). Insert accidentals in the transposed melody to correspond to the altered notes in the given melody.
5) Indicate each diatonic alteration by means of a slashed numeral.
6) Play the transposed melody.

Solution:

Notice that the type of accidental used to raise a scale degree is not necessarily the same in each key. For example, the raised submediant of D- is B *natural* whereas the raised submediant of F♯- is D *sharp*.

Transposing Minor Mode Melodies Containing Chromatic Notes

When transposing a minor mode melody containing chromatic notes, indicate each chromatic alteration in the given melody as well as in the transposed melody. Circle each chromatic note, then, below the staff, write a numeral "slashed" with an arrow to indicate the scale degree that has been raised or lowered. The transposed melody must contain accidentals that correspond to those in the given melody.

Sample Question: Transpose the following melody *down* a major 6th, into the bass clef.

Violin Caprice, Op. 1, No. 15

Solution:

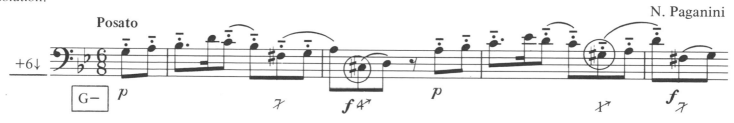

II ⟨EXERCISES ON TRANSPOSITION IN MINOR KEYS⟩

1. For each of the following thematic excerpts:
  (i) name the key;
  (ii) play the excerpt;
  (iii) name the new key and the interval of transposition;
  (iv) transpose the excerpt as instructed;
  (v) play the transposed excerpt.

Prologue from Boris Godunov

a)

up a minor 2nd

Hungarian Rhapsody No. 14

b)

down, into B♭—

Hungarian Dance No. 5

c)

up a perfect 5th

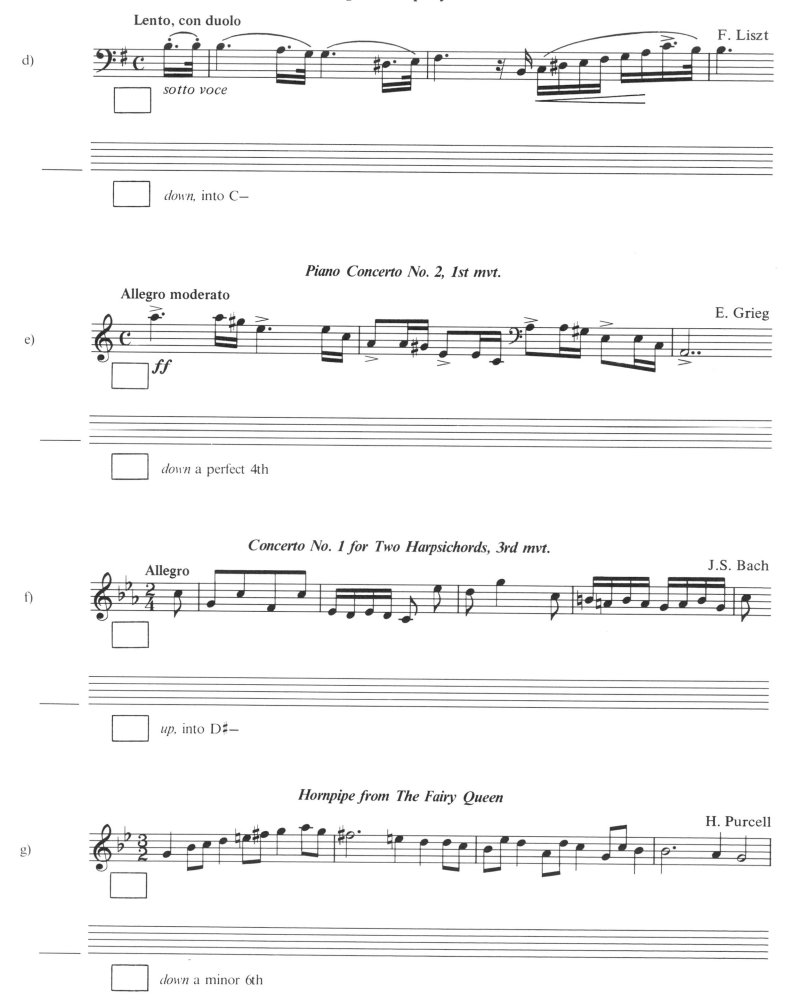

Hungarian Rhapsody No. 5

Lento, con duolo

F. Liszt

d)

sotto voce

down, into C−

Piano Concerto No. 2, 1st mvt.

Allegro moderato

E. Grieg

e)

ff

down a perfect 4th

Concerto No. 1 for Two Harpsichords, 3rd mvt.

J.S. Bach

Allegro

f)

up, into D♯−

Hornpipe from The Fairy Queen

H. Purcell

g)

down a minor 6th

2. For each of the following thematic excerpts:
  (i) name the key;
  (ii) play the excerpt;
  (iii) label each *diatonic* note containing an accidental;
  (iv) circle each *chromatic* note and write a "slashed" numeral beneath it to indicate the scale degree that has been raised or lowered;
  (v) name the new key and the interval of transposition;
  (vi) transpose the excerpt as instructed, indicating each diatonic and chromatic alteration;
  (vii) play the transposed excerpt.

Symphony No. 4 ("Tragic"), 2nd mvt.

F. Schubert

a)

down, into B♭—

Violin Sonata No. 1, 3rd mvt.

R. Schumann

b)

down a minor 3rd

Piano Concerto No. 1, 3rd mvt.

S. Rachmaninoff

c)

up, into C♯—

TRANSPOSING INSTRUMENTS

A *transposing instrument* is one whose notes sound *higher* or *lower* than written. The transposition is calculated in relation to the note C. An instrument in F, for example, sounds F when a written C is played. The actual sound heard by the listener is called *concert pitch*.

Instruments That Sound an Octave Higher or Lower Than Written

Parts for certain instruments that play in a very high or very low register are written in an octave other than that in which they sound. Notating such parts in this way improves readability because it eliminates a large number of ledger lines. For example, music for the double bass is written in the bass clef, one octave *higher* than the instrument sounds.

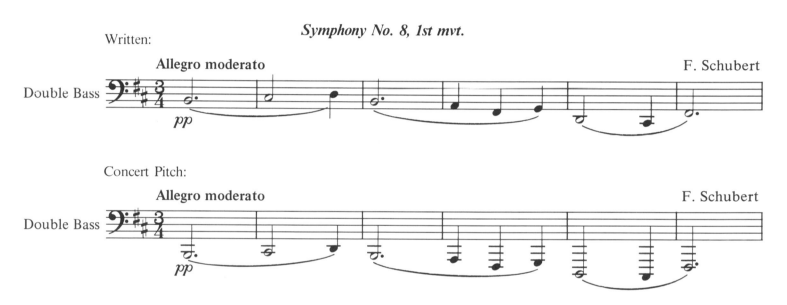

The piccolo sounds in a very high register. If its part were notated at concert pitch, many ledger lines would be required. Music for the piccolo is written in the treble clef, one octave *lower* than the instrument sounds.

Instruments That Sound in a Key Lower Than Written

Some wind instruments are constructed in such a way that they do not sound C when a written C is played. For example, B♭ clarinets and B♭ trumpets sound B♭ when they play a written C. In fact, *all* notes played by a B♭ instrument sound a major 2nd lower than written. It follows, then, that music for a B♭ instrument must be notated a major 2nd *higher* than concert pitch.

Duo for Clarinet and Bassoon, 2nd mvt.

Written:

Concert Pitch:

Notes played by the clarinet in A and the trumpet in A sound a minor 3rd *lower* than written. Notes played by the horn in F and the English horn sound a perfect 5th *lower* than written.

Symphony No. 5, 2nd mvt.

Written:

Concert Pitch:

Instruments That Sound in a Key Higher Than Written

Although the majority of transposing instruments sound in keys lower than written, some sound in keys *higher* than written. An example is the trumpet in D, whose notes sound a major 2nd *higher* than written. When music for a D trumpet is notated in C+, it sounds a major 2nd above the written pitch.

Other examples are the clarinet in E♭ and the trumpet in E♭, whose notes sound a minor 3rd *higher* than written.

Understanding the principle of transposing instruments will enable you to determine concert pitch when you begin to study a score. You must determine both the interval of transposition and whether the music of the transposing instrument sounds higher or lower than written. The key in which the *non*-transposing instruments such as violins are notated in a particular score provides a helpful reference, since parts for these instruments are notated at concert pitch.

To test your understanding of transposing instruments, turn back to the title page of this chapter and determine the concert pitch of the clarinets in A and the horns in F.

O EXERCISES ON TRANSPOSING INSTRUMENTS

1. For each of the following thematic excerpts:
   (i) name the key;
   (ii) name the key in which the excerpt will *sound* when played by the designated instrument;
   (iii) using a key signature, write the excerpt as it will sound (i.e., at concert pitch).

174

C CLEFS

The following are all C clefs:

Soprano   Mezzo-Soprano   Alto   Tenor   Baritone

C clefs tell us where middle C is located on the staff. C clefs were used extensively in older music, mainly in order to avoid ledger lines. However, only two C clefs, the alto clef and the tenor clef, remain in common use today.

II   **The Alto Clef**

The alto clef tells us that middle C is located on the *third* line of the staff.

The alto clef is normally used to notate music for the viola. (When the viola plays in a very high register, the treble clef is used.) The ability to read music in the alto clef is essential for all musicians since the viola is included in the string section of virtually all works in the standard orchestral repertoire. Furthermore, the viola is one of the four instruments in a string quartet and is often a component of other chamber ensembles.

In the alto clef, key signatures appear on the staff as follows:

G+ E−   D+ B−   A+ F♯−   E+ C♯−   B+ G♯−   F♯+ D♯−   C♯+ A♯−

F+ D−   B♭+ G−   E♭+ C−   A♭+ F−   D♭+ B♭−   G♭+ E♭−   C♭+ A♭−

The Tenor Clef

The tenor clef tells us that middle C is located on the *fourth* line of the staff.

The tenor clef is used to notate music for bassoon, cello, and trombone in their upper registers. (The bass clef is used for the middle and lower registers of these instruments.) Musicians must be familiar with the tenor clef in order to read solo or ensemble music written for any of these instruments.

In the tenor clef, key signatures appear on the staff as follows:

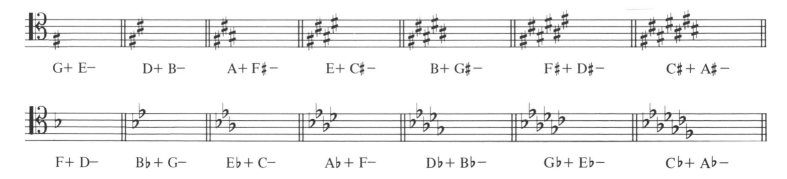

G+ E−   D+ B−   A+ F♯−   E+ C♯−   B+ G♯−   F♯+ D♯−   C♯+ A♯−

F+ D−   B♭+ G−   E♭+ C−   A♭+ F−   D♭+ B♭−   G♭+ E♭−   C♭+ A♭−

Alto Clef Instrumental Piece

Play the viola part of this sonata movement on the piano in order to practise reading music notated in the alto clef. Start on the note B, a minor 2nd *below* middle C, and name the notes as you play them.

Sonata in E Major

François Francœur
(1698-1787)

Tenor Clef Cello Piece

Listen to a performance of this composition for solo cello. Play it on the piano in order to practise reading music notated in the tenor clef.

Sarabande from Cello Suite No. 6

Johann Sebastian Bach
(1685-1750)

II EXERCISES ON C CLEFS

1. Name the keys, then play each of the following scales.

a)

Bb+

b)

☐   harmonic _____

c)

☐

d)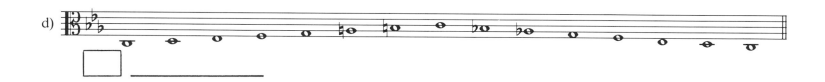

☐ _____

e)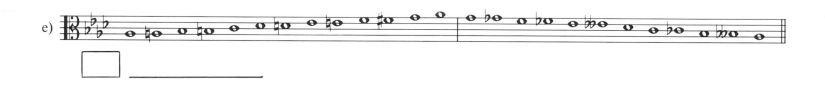

☐ _____

f)

☐

g)

☐ _____

179

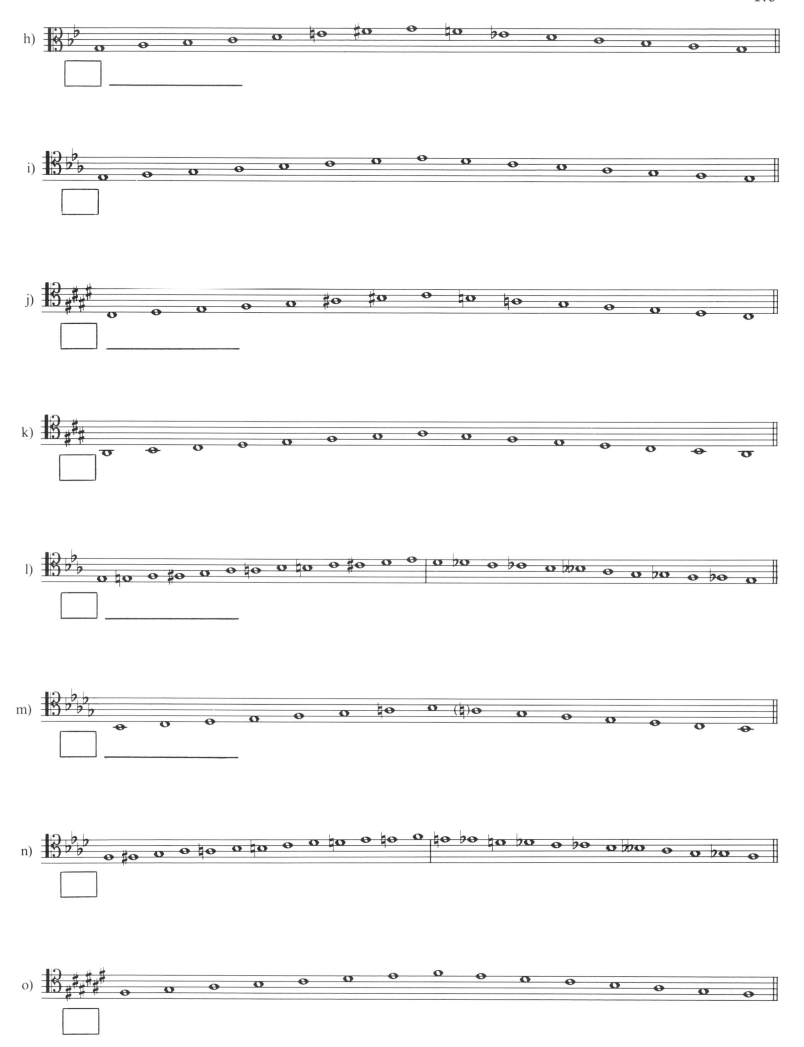

180

2. Write the following scales in the alto clef, using the correct key signature for each.

a)

D♭+, in half notes

b)

C−, in quarter notes

c)

B+, in dotted eighth notes

d)

E− chromatic, in half notes

e)

A♭+, from subdominant to subdominant, in sixteenth notes

f)

E♭− harmonic, in eighth notes

g)

A+ chromatic, in whole notes

h)

B− melodic, in half notes

3. Write the following scales in the tenor clef, using the correct key signature for each.

a)

F– harmonic, in quarter notes

b)

E♭+, from dominant to dominant, in sixteenth notes

c)

B– melodic, in half notes

d)

G+ chromatic, in whole notes

e)

B♭+, from supertonic to supertonic, in dotted quarter notes

f)

G♯– harmonic, in eighth notes

g)

F♯– chromatic, in half notes

h)

B♭ natural minor, in sixteenth notes

182

4. Each of the following excerpts is a viola part from an orchestral score. For each excerpt:
   (i) name the key;
   (ii) name each note;
   (iii) circle any chromatic notes;
   (iv) play the excerpt.

5. Each of the following excerpts is a cello part from an orchestral score. For each excerpt:
   (i) name the key;
   (ii) name each note;
   (iii) circle any chromatic notes;
   (iv) play the excerpt.

6. Analyse the chords in the following excerpt by specifying the root, quality, and position wherever lines are provided.

Symphony No. 7, 2nd mvt.

7. Analyse each boxed chord in the following excerpt by specifying its root, quality, and position.

Sarabande from Cello Suite No. 6

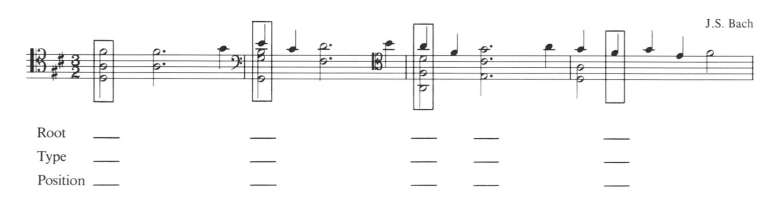

Root ___   ___   ___   ___   ___

Type ___   ___   ___   ___   ___

Position ___   ___   ___   ___   ___

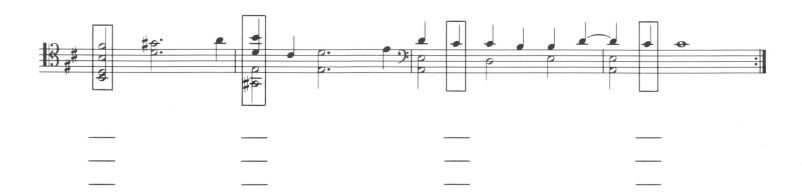

INSTRUMENTAL SCORES

Scores for Instrumental Ensembles

A piece of music written for an orchestra or another group of instruments is called an instrumental score. The score consists of two or more staves joined at the beginning by a continuous vertical line. The staves joined by this line are performed simultaneously, and together they form what is called a *system*. Groups of instruments within the ensemble are indicated by means of a *brace* (}) or a *bracket* ([).

In a printed score, the title of the composition is centered at the top of the first page of music. The composer's name normally appears just above the music, on the right. The tempo marking also appears above the music, but on the left. Instrument names are listed in the margin to the left of the system. These names are most often in Italian, German, or French, and sometimes in English. (A music dictionary will give you the spelling of instrument names in these languages.) Instrument names appear in full next to the first system of music, but are usually abbreviated or omitted on subsequent systems.

Turn back to the title piece of this chapter for an example of an orchestral score.

String Quartet Score

Music written for an ensemble of two violins, viola, and violoncello (cello) is notated in *string quartet score*. In this type of score, the music is written on four staves, one for each part. Each system begins with a bracket and a vertical line, which join all four staves. All bar lines extend vertically through the entire system of four staves. The names of the instruments are written in full or in abbreviated form (Vln I, Vln II, Vla, Vc.) to the left of their respective staves. The treble clef is used to notate both violin parts. The viola part is written in the alto clef, and the cello part is written in the bass clef. As in scores for other instrumental ensembles, the tempo and the composer's name appear just above the first system of music, on the left and right respectively.

Example:

String Quartet No. 15 ("Death and the Maiden"), 2nd mvt.

Observations on string quartet score:

1) All beats of every measure are carefully aligned vertically.

2) Dynamic markings are written separately for each part, usually below the staff.

3) Since there is only one part on a staff, the third line rule applies to *all* stems in *each* part. (When a note is written *above* the third line of any staff, its stem is drawn *downward* from the left side of the notehead. When a note is written *below* the third line, its stem is drawn *upward* from the right side of the notehead. When a note is placed *on* the third line, its stem is normally drawn in whichever direction appears more consistent with the notes surrounding it.)

4) The simultaneous sounding of two notes by a single stringed instrument is called a *double stop*. The two notes of a double stop are written with a single stem, the direction of which is determined by whichever of the two notes is farther from the third line of the staff. (See the second violin part in measures 6 and 7 of the example shown above.)

5) Should slurs or ties appear, they are placed close to the noteheads on the side *opposite* the stems. When two or more notes are slurred and their stems are *not* all written in the same direction, the slur may be placed above or below the notes, whichever looks neater. (Slurred notes appear in the example on page 187.)

Short Score

A string quartet or other instrumental score may be reduced or condensed to a two-stave "short score" for easy reading. The two staves are joined at the left by a brace and a vertical line, and each bar line is drawn through the entire system. The two violin parts are written on the treble staff and the viola and cello parts are written on the bass staff.

Example:

String Quartet No. 15 ("Death and the Maiden"), 2nd mvt.

Observations on short score:

1) When the dynamic levels are the same for all parts, the score includes only *one* set of dynamic markings, written between the staves.

2) Stems for the upper part on each staff are drawn upward, while those for the lower part on each staff are drawn downward.

3) Should the passage contain slurs or ties, those for the upper part on each staff are placed above the notes, while those for the lower part are placed below. (Slurred notes appear in the example on page 187.)

String Quartet and Short Score Transcription

You may be asked to rewrite a short score passage in string quartet score, or vice versa. Study the following sample question and its solution.

Question: Rewrite the following short score excerpt in string quartet score.

Solution:

II EXERCISES ON STRING QUARTET AND SHORT SCORES

1. Rewrite each of the following string quartet score excerpts in short score.

2. Rewrite each of the following short score excerpts in string quartet score.

String Quartet, Op. 18, No. 2, 3rd mvt.

L. van Beethoven

String Quartet, Op. 64, No. 5, 2nd mvt.

F.J. Haydn

CHORAL SCORES

A choral score is a piece of music written for a choir. The standard choral ensemble consists of four parts — soprano, alto, tenor and bass (S.A.T.B.). The term *soprano* refers to a high female voice, the term *alto* to a low female voice. Sopranos sing the highest sounding part in the ensemble, while altos sing the next part below. The term *tenor* refers to a high male voice, the term *bass* to a low male voice. Tenors sing the part below the altos, while basses sing the lowest sounding part in the ensemble. A choral ensemble usually consists of two or more people singing each part.

Short (Reduced) Choral Score

Short choral or *reduced choral* scores are commonly found in hymn books. In this type of score, the music is notated on two staves. The upper staff contains the soprano and alto parts, written in the treble clef, while the lower staff contains the tenor and bass parts, written in the bass clef. The two staves are joined by a brace and a vertical line.

Example:

O Haupt Voll Blut und Wunden

J.S. Bach

Lento

mf O Haupt voll Blut und Wun - den, voll Schmerz und vol - ler Hohn!

Observations on short choral score:

1) If the same text is to be sung by all voices, and if the setting is essentially chordal in style, the score includes only one set of words, written between the staves.
2) Bar lines extend through the five lines of each staff only, so as not to interfere with the words.
3) When the dynamic levels are the same for all parts, the score includes only *one* set of dynamic markings, written between the staves.
4) Stems for the upper part on each staff are drawn upward, and slurs are placed above the notes. Stems for the lower part on each staff are drawn downward, and slurs are placed below the notes.
5) If a phrase ends with a pause for all parts, the score includes only two fermatas: one is placed above the soprano part and the other is placed in inverted form below the bass part.

Modern Vocal Score

Modern vocal score is used nowadays to notate most S.A.T.B. choral music. In this type of score, the music is written on four staves, one for each part. The soprano part is written in the treble clef on the uppermost staff, while the alto part is written in the treble clef on the next staff below. The tenor part appears on the third staff. It is written in the treble clef *one octave higher than it actually sounds.* (Many composers attach a small 8 beneath the treble clef of the tenor part as a reminder that the tenor part is written one octave higher than it sounds.) The bass part is written in the bass clef on the lowest staff of cach system.

Example:

O Haupt Voll Blut und Wunden

Observations on modern vocal score:

1) There are four sets of words, one below each part.
2) A bracket and a vertical line join all four staves at the beginning of each system, but bar lines extend through the five lines of each staff only, so as not to interfere with the words.
3) Dynamic markings are written separately for each part, either consistently above or consistently below the staff.
4) Since there is only one part per staff, the third line rule applies to *all* stems in *each* part.
5) Slurs or ties are placed close to the noteheads on the side opposite the stems. When two or more notes are slurred and their stems are not all written in the same direction, the slur may be placed above or below the notes, whichever looks neater.
6) If a phrase ends with a pause for all parts, the score includes a fermata for each part, written above the note on which the pause occurs.

Old Vocal Score

In *old vocal score,* the alto part is written in the alto clef and the tenor part is written in the tenor clef. The tenor part is written exactly as it sounds and is therefore *not* transposed as it is in modern vocal score. In all other respects, the notation of old vocal score corresponds to that of modern vocal score. Study the following example written in old vocal score.

O Haupt Voll Blut und Wunden

Modern Vocal, Old Vocal, and Short Score Transcription

You may be asked to rewrite one type of vocal score in another type of vocal score. Study the following sample questions and their solutions.

Example 1

Question: Rewrite the following short score excerpt in modern vocal score.

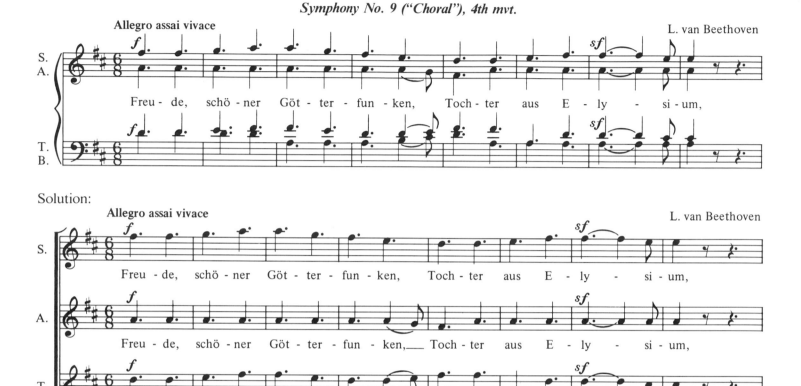

Solution:

Example 2

Question: Rewrite the following old vocal score excerpt in short score.

Solution:

H. Purcell

Hear, might-y Love! to thee I call; Give me As - tre - a, and I have all.

| EXERCISES ON CHORAL SCORES |

1. For each of the following choral excerpts:
  (i) name the type of score given;
  (ii) rewrite the excerpt in the type of score specified.

_____

Ave Verum

W.A. Mozart

a)

A - ve,_____ a - ve   ve - rum_____ cor - pus,

Modern Vocal Score _____

194

b) S.

A.

T.

B.

Short Score

Acis and Galatea

c) S.
A.

T.
B.

Old Vocal Score

The Creation

F.J. Haydn

Allegro

d) S.

The heav - ens are tell - ing the glo - ry of God,____

A.

The heav - ens are tell - ing the glo - ry of God,

T.

The heav - ens are tell - ing the glo - ry of God,____

B.

The heav - ens are tell - ing the glo - ry of God,

Short Score

Acis and Galatea

G.F. Handel

Allegro

e) S.

Hap - py, hap - py, hap - py, hap - py, hap - py, hap - py, hap - py we,

A.

Hap - py, hap - py, hap - py, hap - py, hap - py, hap - py, hap - py we,

T.

Hap - py, hap - py, hap - py,__ hap - py, hap - py, hap - py, hap - py we,

B.

Hap - py, hap - py, hap - py, hap - py, hap - py, hap - py, hap - py we,

Old Vocal Score